Rev. John R. Morris, O.P.
PM Box 3042
1928 Saint Mary's Road
Moraga, CA 94575

SACRAMENTAL THEOLOGY

Fifty Years After Vatican II

Kenan B. Osborne, O.F.M.

lecțio

Lectio Publishing, LLC

Hobe Sound, FL
Cincinnati, OH

www.lectiopublishing.com

Cover design by Linda Wolf
Edited by Leah Wolf

ISBN 978-0-9898397-3-0

Library of Congress Control Number: 2014931175

Published by Lectio Publishing, LLC

Hobe Sound, Florida 33455

www.lectiopublishing.com

Printed and bound in the United States of America

Table of Contents

INTRODUCTION
Vatican II And Sacramental Renewal   vii

CHAPTER ONE
Sacramental Theology Today: 50 Years After Vatican II   1

I. Christ, the Sacrament of the Encounter with God   2

II. The Church as the Original Sacrament   4

III. The Church is the Basic Sacrament   9

IV. Sacraments are the Work of the Holy Trinity   15

    An Analysis of Section One: "The Sacramental Economy"   16

V. The Seven Sacraments of the Church   27

    1. The Naming of Baptism, the Sacrament of Initiation   29

    2. The Sacrament of Confirmation, a Sacrament of Initiation   34

    3. The Sacrament of the Eucharist, a Sacrament of Initiation 36

    4. The Sacrament of Penance, a Sacrament of Healing   40

    5. The Sacrament of the Anointing of the Sick, a Sacrament
       of Healing   44

    6. The Sacrament of Holy Orders, a Sacrament at the
       Service of Communion   48

    7. The Sacrament of Matrimony, a Sacrament of Service
       and Communion   50

VI. Conclusions   52

CHAPTER TWO
Sacramental Theology within the Three Western
Theological Traditions   63

I. The Role of the Three Major Theological Traditions in the Western

Roman Catholic Church   66

   Stage One: The Beginning of an Intellectual Tradition   72

   Stage Two: The Initial Steps of an Intellectual Tradition   72

   Stage Three: The Slow but Sure Growth of the Founder's Positions   73

   Stage Four: The Academic Acceptance of an Intellectual Tradition   73

II. The Augustinian Theological Tradition   75

   1. The Life of Augustine (354-430)   75

   2. The Immediate Followers of Saint Augustine   76

   3. The Theological Tradition of Augustine Begins to Show Signs of a Permanent Tradition   76

   4. The Augustinian Theological and Philosophical Tradition Becomes an Intrinsic Part of Western Church Thinking   77

III. The Thomistic Theological Tradition   79

   1. The Thomistic tradition has carefully structured its theological material within an Aristotelian philosophical base.   81

   2. The Thomistic tradition has presented the church with a "Summa of Created Life," namely a life which has come from a loving and creator God.   82

   3. The Thomistic tradition has provided the Catholic Church with a unity of philosophical insights and theological beliefs within a coherent program, and from Reformation times on, this unified doctrine has provided the Catholic Church with a strongly unified intellectual framework, which became a strong bulwark in its stance toward Anglican, Protestant, and Free Church theologies.   83

IV. The Franciscan Theological Tradition   87

   1. The Title of the Tradition, namely, the "Franciscan Tradition"   87

   2. The Franciscan Theology of a Trinitarian God   88

   3. The Franciscan Emphasis on the Infinity of God as

expressed in the Theology of John Duns Scotus 90

V. Conclusions 95

CHAPTER THREE
The History of Sacramental Theology From 1896 to 2014 107

I. An Overview of the Development of the History of the
Sacraments from 1896 to 2014 111

  1. The history of the sacraments has raised a major
question: Did Jesus institute all seven sacraments
during his lifetime? 113

  2. A New Evaluation of the Tridentate Statement
"Anathema Sit" 116

II. The References to the History of the Sacraments in the
Documents of Vatican II 119

  The Introductory Paragraphs of *Sacrosanctum Concilium*

120

  Chapter One of *Sacrosanctum Concilium* 121

III. The References to the History of the Sacraments in the
Catechism of the Catholic Church 125

  Baptism and Confirmation 125

  Eucharist 126

  Reconciliation 128

  Anointing of the Sick 129

  Holy Orders 130

  Matrimony 131

IV. Conclusions 133

CHAPTER FOUR
The Liturgy – Work of the Holy Spirit 143

I. Preliminary Observations Regarding the Background and Goals
of Chapter Four 144

1. The Designation of the Humanity of Jesus as a
   Foundational Sacrament   145

2. The Designation of the Church as a Foundational
   Sacrament   146

3. The Official Designation of the Church as a
   Foundational Sacrament   148

4. The Designation of Sacramental Life as the Work of the
   Trinity   152

5. The Presentation of the Seven Sacraments as Found in
   the *Catechism*   153

6. There is a major caveat that remains even today. It is not
   fully developed, but it is central to the very meaning
   of sacrament.   154

II. Which Understanding of the Trinity is at Work in Contemporary
Literature's Presentation of Sacramental Theology?   156

1. The Augustinian Understanding of Trinity   157

2. The Thomistic Understanding of Trinity   160

3. The Franciscan Understanding of the Trinity   162

III. A Sacramental Theology for Today – The Work of the Holy
Trinity   166

IV. Conclusions   181

APPENDIX
The Theology of Salvation   **187**

Bibliography   **197**

INTRODUCTION

Vatican II And Sacramental Renewal

From 1962 to 1965, the Second Vatican Council was in session. From 2012 to 2015, the Catholic Church is celebrating fifty-years after the Second Vatican Council. To honor these fifty years, many books and articles have already been written and other books and articles will be written in the years to come. These volumes have traced major issues that the bishops at Vatican II promulgated, and they have described the development or non-development of these major issues during the past fifty years.

The most influential change the bishops at Vatican II made was the change in a theology of church. However, a change in the theology of church cannot avoid changing, at least in a secondary way, both the theological meaning of sacraments and the liturgical celebration of the Christian sacraments. In other words, the theology of the church in a major way and the theology of sacraments in a secondary way have been reconstructed in and through the documents of the second Vatican Council.

The conciliar bishops enriched the theological meaning of church through a number of major documents, and this new meaning of church has changed both the meaning and the celebration of the sacraments. The following outlines the changes in both church and sacrament through each document.

1. The Dogmatic Constitution on the Church, *Lumen Gentium*

In this major document, the church was presented as a sacrament of Jesus, who is the light of the world, *Lumen Gentium*. Naming the church as a foundational sacrament has engendered a new theology of the church and of the seven ritualized sacraments. This change in ecclesiology could be described as the most radical change the bishops made during the years of the council.

2. The Constitution on the Sacred Liturgy, *Sacrosanctum Concilium*

In chapter one of *Sacrosanctum Concilium*, the bishops present Jesus Christ as the basis for the life of the church. The church, as a foundational sacrament of Christ, has subsequently reformulated the pre-Vatican II theology of the seven liturgical sacraments. Consequently, the sacramentality of the church itself is the necessary starting point for the theology of the seven liturgical sacraments (§§5-13). This is a new starting point for sacramental liturgy.

In this document, the bishops also established norms for liturgical celebrations (§§21-46). These norms, which cover many liturgical situations, can be considered to be the second major achievement of the Vatican II documents. The opening paragraphs of these norms state a caveat (§§22-23), which focuses on the issue of religious leadership. For the Catholic faith, the final approval rests with the Apostolic See and with various groupings of bishops. However, *Sacrosanctum Concilium* states that the major traditions of the Catholic Church should be honored by both those in authority and by those who are in the wider Catholic community.

In the norms, a new step was taken by the bishops at Vatican II when they clearly called for a revision of the liturgical books (§25). The document states that well-trained liturgical experts should be employed for this task and that bishops from various parts of the world should be consulted. The bishops also emphasize that sacred scripture should be a central part in every revision of the sacramental liturgies (§24). Moreover, in the sacramental liturgies the bishops ask that a greater communal participation should be established (§37). As we shall see in chapter one, it is the *Christus totus*, Jesus and the whole church community, who celebrate sacramental liturgies. The bishops also wanted each and every revision to be focused in ways that will deepen the spirituality of the women and men who are present at sacramental celebrations (§26). Finally, in a remarkable section of these regulations, the bishops clearly opened the liturgy of the church to diverse forms of multi-cultural liturgical celebrations (§§37-40).

The conciliar bishops established general norms in detail regarding the celebration of the sacraments (§§21-46), and from §47 to the end of the document, many other norms and regulations were established as well. In Chapter II (§§47-58), the norms expressed the need to involve the total community whenever the sacred mystery of the Eucharist is celebrated. Eucharistic celebrations can only be a meaningful event when the rites are simplified. In Chapter III (§§59-82), the bishops focused on the other sacraments and on sacramentals. These, too, need a revision so as to make them more meaningful to the laity. In Chapter III, the bishops once again call for an opening of the liturgies to various cultures and so they become multi-cultural celebrations instead of only Euro-American. In Chapter IV (§§83-101), the bishops provide norms for revising the Divine Office in order to make it a more prayerful celebration. In Chapter V (§§102-121), the bishops provide norms for the Liturgical Year. In the final two chapters (§§112-130), they establish norms for sacred music and sacred art.

All of these norms were meant to be put into practice by the leadership of the church, once the council was concluded. In general, church leadership has followed these norms, but there have also been some major modifications of these norms. The liturgical norms regarding the sacraments have restructured the pre-Vatican II liturgical norms that were strongly based on Neo-Scholastic theology. The new liturgical norms envision Christian women and men celebrating all the sacraments together with Jesus, thereby opening the liturgy to new forms of lay ministry.

These norms are based on a renewed view of ecclesiology, in which the leadership of the Catholic Church should be open to liturgical adaptations vis-à-vis the many cultural temperaments and traditions of today's Catholic world. The norms for cultural adaptation in *Sacrosanctum Concilium* even make allowance for radical adaptations of the liturgy. The Latin text and its English translation for radical liturgical adaptation read as follows:

> Cum tamen in variis locis et adiunctis, profundior Liturgiae aptatio urgeat, et ideo difficilior evadat.

> In some places and circumstances, however, an even more radical adaptation of the liturgy is needed, and this entails greater difficulties (§40).

The bishops offer three distinct norms to guide the radical or more profound cultural adaptations in liturgical celebrations. First of all, the norms for a radical change require the endorsement of the territorial bishops after they have adequately studied the reasons for a radical liturgical change. If the territorial bishops consider the radical changes to be necessary, the territorial bishops should then send their recommendations to the Apostolic See. At this second stage, the Apostolic See can agree or not agree to the more profound or radical changes, but if it does agree to the changes, it should set a time-limit on the exercise of the more radical liturgical adaptations. The third norm states that experts in the study of mission lands should be consulted throughout this process.

Under John Paul II and Benedict XVI, radical adaptations that territorial bishops asked for were generally denied because both popes wanted to maintain the status quo. Nonetheless, we see in the cultural norms regarding radical liturgical change a major step forward for a theology of today's multicultural church. The new ecclesiology is no longer meant to be Euro-American. Rather, the new ecclesiology is meant to be multicultural, even if this means radical changes in liturgical celebrations.

3. The Pastoral Constitution, *Gaudium et Spes*

Gaudium et Spes is a singularly important document for understanding the contemporary Catholic Church. The bishops at Vatican II, for the most part, did not want to reiterate the theology of the church that Vatican I had presented. Rather, the bishops at Vatican II strongly wanted to present a Catholic Church that could exist positively and encouragingly in the late twentieth-century world. In this document, the bishops carefully opened structures of the church to today's multi-faceted world. Consequently, the newly-formed contours of a multi-faceted world church have called for a multi-faceted sacramental church which is open to today's world. A change in ecclesiology unavoidably means a change in sacramental theology.

4. The Decree on the Catholic Eastern Churches, *Orientalium Ecclesiarum*

In the decree on the Catholic Eastern Churches, *Orientalium Ecclesiarum*, the windows and doors of the Catholic Western Church have been opened for a richer and a more positive acceptance of communication and cooperation with the Eastern Catholic Churches. Through the communication and cooperation with these Churches, a deeper and more thorough theological understanding of the sacraments has begun to appear. The liturgies of the Eastern Catholic Churches reflect the ecclesiology of these same churches, and Roman Catholics can now study this Orthodox relationship and perhaps make changes in western forms of both ecclesiology and the theology of sacraments.

5. The Decree on Ecumenism, *Unitatis Redintegratio*

In the decree on ecumenism, respect for other forms of Christianity was given a positive presentation. The openness of the Catholic Church to the ecumenical movement has helped, in some degree, to heal the sacramental differences between the Roman Christian Church and the various non-Roman Christian Churches of the west. The issues of the theology of sacraments and of the celebration of sacraments have become key themes in contemporary ecumenical discussions. The World Council of Churches has used the Lima Document as a means of inter-denominational reference, and the replies to the Lima Document from various denominations have had many positive results.

6. The Declaration on Religious Liberty, *Dignitatis Humanae*

The declaration on religious liberty, *Dignitatis Humanae*, increases respect for the personal integrity of Catholics and respect for the religious integrity of others. Religious liberty for Christian men and women has certainly helped the leaders of the Catholic Church to hear the needs of the laity in a more profound and over-arching way. With the renewal of the sacraments, Catholics who had not found answers to their needs in the pre-Vatican II sacramental celebrations have begun to discover a renewed integrity of gospel living through liturgical services.

7. The Decree on Missionary Activity, *Ad Gentes Divinitus*, and the Decree on Non-Christian Religions, *Nostra Aetate*

In the decree on missionary activity, *Ad Gentes Divinitus*, and in the decree on non-Christian religions, *Nostra Aetate*, the holiness of other religions has been carefully but hesitantly acknowledged. In an inchoative way, but also in an enriching way, these documents have affected sacramental liturgy, since any major change in ecclesiology has an effect on the theology of the sacraments.

Although liturgy and sacraments are mentioned in almost every document of Vatican II, the Constitution on the Sacred Liturgy, *Sacrosanctum Concilium*, is the major conciliar document that guides the renewal of the Church's sacramental life. In *Sacrosanctum Concilium*, the bishops established norms for the reform of the sacred liturgy that are a clear call for sacramental renewal on a large scale.

While writing this book, I kept the document, *Sacrosanctum Concilium*, on one side of my desk, and on the other side of my desk I kept a major pre-Vatican II theological textbook that dealt with the Neo-Scholastic theology of sacraments, which I selected with special care. I wanted to clearly see the differences between the approaches to the sacraments as presented in the Vatican II document on the liturgy on the one hand, and on the other hand I wanted to see the Neo-Scholastic formulation of liturgy.

The book that I chose was written in 1962, the same year in which Vatican II began. Several Jesuit professors at the University of Salamanca published a four-volume manual of theology. In many ways, these four volumes presented a thorough and profound explanation of the Neo-Scholastic theology. In volume four, the Jesuit authors, Joseph Aldama, Richardo Franco, Severino González, and Francisco Solá developed a detailed and well-referenced theology of the sacraments. In my view, this volume on sacramental life is one of the best Neo Scholastic theological textbooks ever written.

A similar book on Neo-Scholastic sacraments will never be written again after Vatican II because the documents of Vatican II and the writings of various sacramental theologians after Vatican II have changed sacramental theology in major ways. When I moved my focus from the constitution on the liturgy regarding certain aspects of sacramental life to the Neo-Scholastic theological volume and its presentation of sacramental life, I was able to see more clearly the differences between then and now.

In the following pages, I will present the major sacramental changes from the documents of Vatican II in a summarized way. However, we should first consider these questions: why are there changes? Isn't the Catholic Church basically unchangeable? The answer to these questions can be stated in a clear way.

From the early 1800s down to the opening of Vatican II, there was a strong movement in the Roman Catholic Church for a reconsideration of ecclesiology.[1] The bishops at Vatican II were well aware of this century-long desire for a re-examination of the theology of church.

With the approval of Pope Pius XII, a committee of major theologians began to restructure both the theology and the liturgy of Holy Week. In 1951, their efforts were officially approved by Pius XII.

Pius XII had also constituted a "secret committee," which studied the history of the liturgy in great detail. Over several years of consultation, this committee had gathered together an abundance of material on the history of Roman Catholic liturgy. Consequently, the bishops and periti at Vatican II had readily available access to this data, which was needed for constructing the sacred constitution on the liturgy, *Sacrosanctum Concilium*, and for providing background for liturgical renewal. Consequently, the first document the bishops at Vatican II issued was the document on liturgy.

Fourthly, in the immediate years just prior to Vatican II, several well-known theologians published key volumes on the sacraments. Among these authors were Edward Schillebeeckx, Otto Semmelroth, and Karl Rahner. Many of the bishops at Vatican II had read these theological works, and thus were prepared to reconsider sacramental life within the Catholic Church.

Given this strong antecedent background of theological and liturgical investigation of ecclesiology, the bishops were able, from the very start of the council, to focus on the spiritual and theological meaning of Church.[2]

The documents of Vatican II officially endorsed a new theological view of the Church. Namely, that the church itself is the foundational sacrament. Thirty-two years after Vatican II, the leaders of the church presented us with a newly revised *Catechism of the Catholic Church*. This new catechism is strongly based on the documents of Vatican II. In the *Catechism of the Catholic Church*, sacramental theology is presented in two forms. In the first form (§§1076-1209), sacramental liturgy is presented as the work of the Holy Trinity and the ministers of every sacramental celebration are Jesus and the Christian community, the *Christus totus*. In the second form (§§1210-1066), the *Catechism* offers us a post-conciliar attempt to unite the Neo-Scholastic theology of sacraments with insights found in the documents of Vatican II. As we shall see, this second section is in many ways a step-backward rather than a step forward.

During the fifty years after Vatican II, the Christian communities were not offered only one new form of sacramental renewal. Rather, the communities today have been given five different theologies of sacramental life. All five of these sacramental theologies have the approval of church leadership, and all five theologies are still being more deeply developed by qualified theologians, liturgists, and scholars of church history. The five differing sacramental theologies will continue to produce more insights and values in the next few decades. We are in a time of change and we will continue to be in change as we move toward new sacramental horizons.

In this volume I will present, as clearly and honestly as I can, the five differing theologies of sacramental life that are found in the Vatican II documents, in the writings of major theologians, and in the *Catechism of the Catholic Church*. However, in chapter four I will offer a more thorough analysis of one of these five choices which I perceive to have the most lasting qualities and the deepest meaning of sacramental life.

During the past fifty years, theological and liturgical changes regarding of sacramental life have encountered both progressive and conservative Christians. These conflicting situations have had, to some degree, a very encouraging presence, since both the progressive parties and the conservative parties have had to restudy the history of sacramental theology from the first century through today. Both parties have had to restudy not only sacramental theology in its historical development, but also the histories of ecclesiology, Christology, and the theology of a Trinitarian God, which form the foundation of any and every sacramental theology.

Because of all the developments mentioned above, the structure of this volume is divided into five chapters.

In chapter one, *Sacramental Theology Today: Fifty Years After Vatican II*, I present in detail the five ways in which the theology of sacraments has been changed since Vatican II. Naturally, these five changes had their roots in theological research prior to Vatican II, but these five approaches to sacramental life have developed more carefully in the past fifty years, each in its own way.

In chapter two, *Sacramental Theology within the Three Western Theological Traditions*, I will present in detail the three main theological traditions within the western Catholic Church. As we shall see in this chapter, almost every major western Catholic theology since the seventh century has been formulated within the framework of a particular theological tradition. The first tradition was the Augustinian tradition which, as a tradition, began in the sixth and seventh centuries. In the thirteenth and fourteenth centuries, two more traditions were developed: the Thomistic tradition and the Franciscan tradition. Even today, in a post-Vatican II Christian world, the majority of Catholic theologians are still theologizing in and through one of these three theological traditions.

In chapter three, *The History of the Seven Sacraments of the Catholic Church*, I review the tremendous amount of historical research on the history of the seven sacraments, which began in 1896 and has continued through the present. The history of each sacrament has called into question very sensitive positions, such as: did Jesus Christ institute the seven sacraments of the Catholic Church during his life or in his appearances after the resurrection? Did the apostolic church of the first and second centuries have all seven sacraments? Has each of the seven sacraments been celebrated in the same way that we celebrate these sacraments today? The vast material of the history of the sacraments, which has been richly developed in the past one hundred years, appears to have little to no effect on the official statements on sacraments emanating from the Apostolic See and the conferences of bishops.

The conciliar bishops at Vatican II, for their part, did not enter into the historical development of the sacraments. I believe they had good reasons for not doing so. Vatican II was not a council focused on the sacraments. Rather, it was a council focused on the theological and spiritual meaning of the Catholic Church. Consequently, the history of the sacraments was not part of the bishops' agenda.

In the *Catechism of the Catholic Church*, there are a few references to the history of the sacraments. However, these are mentioned rarely and they often appear in small type, which indicates that the authors of the *Catechism* considered the material to be secondary. This issue will also be discussed in chapter three.

In chapter four, *The Liturgy – Work of the Holy Trinity*, I have selected one of the five post-Vatican II forms of sacramental theology to develop in detail. In my view, this form of sacramental theology has a promising future for a contemporary discussion of sacramental life in the Catholic Church.

I am deeply indebted to the friars of the Franciscan Province of St. Barbara for their support of my academic career over many, many years. In a very special way, I am grateful for the many professors and students at the Franciscan School of Theology and at the sister schools that form the Graduate Theological Union. The intellectual framework of the schools in Berkeley has consistently urged me to continue studying, researching, and renewing my understanding of both theology and philosophy.

I am also deeply indebted to Lectio Publishing, LLC. Its editorial staff has been very encouraging during the composition of this book. I am honored to be one of the early authors of this new religious publishing company.

Hopefully, sacramental grace will continue to strengthen Christian women and men in a strong way as we Christians move more deeply into the twenty-first century and into our sacramental life.

Endnotes

1. In my volume, *A Theology of the Church for the Third Millennium: A Franciscan Approach* (Leiden: Brill, 2009), I provide a detailed analysis regarding the call for a change in Roman Catholic ecclesiology from the sixteenth century down to the present, pp. ix to 127. All of this material indicates that a change in ecclesiology was a major cause for the call of the Vatican II Council.

2. Vatican II had a very dramatic beginning. On Saturday, October 13, 1962, the bishops gathered for the first business session, officially called the first General Congregation. Cardinal Tisserant was the president, and the first item on the agenda was his call to elect the members of the ten conciliar commissions. The agenda for these conciliar commissions was to draft proposals for the decrees. As soon as the Secretary General, Pericle Cardinal Felici, announced that the Council would proceed to the election, Achille Cardinal Liénart rose and read a prepared statement in which he suggested that the bishops would not proceed immediately with the elections but that they would have time to meet together in national and regional groupings and draw up possible members for the conciliar commissions. Cardinal Frings of Cologne seconded the proposal. After some few minutes of discussion Cardinal Tisserant adjourned the meeting. This opening meeting of Vatican II lasted for about twenty-five minutes, but in that space of time it was made clear to the conservative bishops that they were not the main directors of Vatican II. The struggle between the conservative bishops, led by the bishops of the Vatican Curia, and the more open bishops continued during most of the conciliar sessions. See, Melissa J. Wilde, *Vatican II: A Sociological Analysis of Religious Change* (Princeton, NJ: Princeton University Press, 2007), 17-20.

CHAPTER ONE

Sacramental Theology Today: 50 Years After Vatican II

In the fifty years since the Second Vatican Council, five major theological positions have developed regarding Roman Catholic theology of sacraments. These developments have changed both the theology and the practice of Catholic sacramental life. The five positions, however, are not uniform. Each of the changes moves in a different theological direction. As a result, in today's Catholic Church there are five different formats of sacramental theology, and all five are ecclesiastically acceptable positions. The subject of the first chapter, accordingly, is an explanation of these five forms of sacramental theology.

Chapter one is divided into six parts.

I. *Christ, the Sacrament of the Encounter with God*. This position was presented by Edward Schillebeeckx in 1960.

II. *The Church as the Original Sacrament*. This position was presented by Otto Semmelroth in 1960 and then in a more developed way by Karl Rahner in 1961.

III. *The Church is the Basic Sacrament*. This position is found in the documents of Vatican II (LG, 1, 9, and 48; GS, 45; SC 2 and 5; and AG 5).

IV. *Sacraments are the Work of the Holy Trinity*. This position is found in the *Catechism of the Catholic Church* (§§ 1076-1209).

V. *The Seven Sacraments of the Church*. This position is found in the *Catechism of the Catholic Church* (§§ 1210-1666).

VI. *Conclusions*.

I. Christ, the Sacrament of the Encounter with God

In 1960, the Dominican theologian, Edward Schillebeeckx, published a volume entitled *Christus: Sacrament van de Godsonmoeting.*[1] This volume was quickly translated into many languages and became very popular throughout the Catholic world. Cornelius Ernst translated the book into English: *Christ the Sacrament of the Encounter with God.*[2]

In his volume, Schillebeeckx presents the human nature of Jesus as the primary sacrament. The divine nature of Jesus is not and cannot be a part of Jesus as sacrament, since the divine nature of God is totally perfect in itself. The human nature of Jesus is created and limited, and therefore it can be described in a sacramental way.

Two basic questions immediately arise in every sacrament. The first question is "the sacrament of what?" And the second question is: "for whom is this a sacrament?" Asking "of what?" and "for whom?" clarifies what a given sacrament expresses and implies. When one states that the human nature of Jesus is a sacrament, these two questions are of great importance; of what is the human nature of Jesus a sacrament, and for whom is the human nature of Jesus a sacrament?

The human nature of Jesus is a "sacrament of God's own nature," for his human nature reflects the presence of God. The reflection of God in the human nature of Jesus is limited, since a human nature, even the human nature of Jesus, is limited.

The human nature of Jesus is a "sacrament for all men and women." God's sending of the Logos is manifested in the human nature of the Logos. This reflection of God in the human nature of Jesus is limited, since a human nature, even the human nature of Jesus, is limited; therefore many women and men in this world might not understand the sacramentality of Jesus' human nature.

We read in the gospels that Jesus' disciples and the Jewish people at large asked a number of questions: who is this Jesus? Is he the prophet who comes at the end time? Is he a teacher of the sacred writings of Judaism? Is he the messiah? These and other questions appear again and again in the four gospels.[3] The "who is Jesus" questions correspond to the "of what?" is Jesus, in his human nature, as a sacrament. These questions also imply the "for whom?" aspect of Jesus, and in the gospels we find men and women who accept Jesus as a reflection of God and we find men and women who reject Jesus as a messenger of God.

After the resurrection, the gospels indicate a profound acceptance of Jesus as the sacrament of God. One of the most dramatic instances of this acceptance "of Jesus" and "for whom" is found in the words of the doubting Thomas: "My Lord and my God" (Jn. 20:28).

Schillebeeckx carefully presents his position that Jesus of Nazareth is the sacrament of our encounter with God. He writes:

> The dogmatic definition of Chalcedon, according to which Christ in "one person in two natures," implies that one and the same person, the Son of God, also took on a visible human form. Even in his humanity Christ is the Son of God. The second person of the most holy Trinity is personally man; and this man is personally God.[4]

For Schillebeeckx, the divine Logos is not a sacrament. The humanity of Jesus alone can be seen as a primordial sacrament. He carefully presents his case:

> The man Jesus, as the personal visible realization of the divine grace of redemption, is the sacrament, the primordial sacrament, because this man, the Son of God himself, in intended by the Father to be in his humanity the only way to the actuality of redemption.[5]

In Schillebeeckx's theological position, he is asking of what is the humanity of Jesus a sacrament, and for whom is the humanity of Jesus a sacrament? Schillebeeckx clearly states his answers to these two questions: the humanity of Jesus is the sacrament *of* God's grace of redemption *for* all men and women.

The bishops at Vatican II did not present the humanity of Jesus as the primordial sacrament or the *Ursakrament*. Nor did they specifically present the church as the primordial sacrament or the *Ursakrament*, a term that does not occur in any of the Vatican II documents. They did, however, clearly present the church as a sacrament in and through which the seven sacraments have their meaning. On the other hand, no church authority has yet challenged the theological approach of Schillebeeckx on its understanding of the humanity of Jesus as a primordial sacrament.[6] Schillebeeckx's position on Jesus the primordial sacrament continues, among some theologians, to be a profound approach to the sacramental economy precisely because of its centering in the incarnate Logos.[7]

II. The Church as the Original Sacrament

In 1959, the Jesuit theologian Otto Semmelroth delivered a series of lectures sponsored by the Catholic Academic Association at the University of Bonn in Germany. The following year, 1960, he published a book based on his lectures entitled *Vom Sinn der Sakramente*, which was translated into English five years later as *Church and Sacrament*.[8] In this book, Semmelroth frequently states that the church is a sacrament. For instance, he writes:

> "An explanation of the visible Church as sacramental sign."[9]

> "The understanding of the sacramental mystery of the Church ..."[10]

> "The Church as a Sacramental Sign."[11]

> "We have discussed the Church as a sacramental sign of salvation."[12]

> "The Church is a symbolic or sacramental image, a sign from

which we can read the essential structure of the salvation-event."[13]

The Vatican Offices have never questioned Semmelroth's description of the church as the basic sacrament in and through which the ritual sacraments find their rootage. In his book, Semmelroth does not indicate that the meaning of sacrament when applied to the church differs from the meaning of sacrament when applied to the seven rituals. For Semmelroth, the church is fundamentally a sign or sacrament of God's plan of salvation in and through the incarnate Jesus, and Semmelroth also states that the church as sacrament is the base that makes the seven sacraments meaningful.

As a result, his book focuses heavily on the sacramentality of the church. Ecclesiology, therefore, is the centering theme of his book. He notes that there were misconceptions about the theology of church in the writings of some Catholic theologians. Semmelroth takes to task the conception of church as a community of individuals with an emphasis on individuality and he challenges the conception of church as only a collective group of believers. Semmelroth argues that both of these misconceptions do an injustice to the true meaning of church.[14]

To offset these misconceptions, Semmelroth presents his thesis that the church is a three-dimensional reality which consists of a vertical dimension, a dimension of depth, and a horizontal dimension.[15] The vertical dimension is basically God's gratuitous gift of salvation. The dimension of depth is the community called church reaching out to God. The horizontal dimension involves the church's entire spectrum of social existence.

On the basis of these three dimensions, Semmelroth explains how the church itself is a sacramental sign.[16] The author's goal of this volume is clearly stated in the Foreword:

> One must know how the proclamation of the word of God
> and the sacramental worship are intended by the God-man
> founder as the many-in-one form of the Church's life. The
> sacramental-life-functions themselves are rightly under-
> stood only from the perspective of the sacramental mystery
> of the Church whose actualization they are. One must recog-
> nize the meaning of the Church as a sign of salvation insti-
> tuted by Christ.[17]

In the section on the church as a sacramental sign, Semmelroth
develops the details of his position. In this explanation, he presents the
two complementary elements of the church, namely, clergy and laity.
On the basis of a clerical-lay church, he then moves to the seven sacramental rituals. These rituals are sacramental because they are based on
the church itself, which is a foundational sacramental sign.

Semmelroth's book was read primarily by trained theologians.
Even though it was translated into other languages, the book remained
a volume which the ordinary lay man or lay woman did not read. Its
influence, therefore, remained within the confines of the theological
and academic world.

In 1963, Karl Rahner published his volume on the sacraments,
Kirche und Sakramente. In the same year, an English translation by W.
J. O'Hara appeared under the title *The Church and the Sacraments*.[18] In
his book, Rahner does not cite Semmelroth. In fact, his citations of any
theologians are quite meager throughout the book. However, in Rahner's article, "Zur Theologie des Symbols," he does cite Semmelroth
and many other theologians.[19] In this article, Rahner even describes
the church as the primordial sacrament, *Ursakrament*.

In the preface, Rahner reminds the reader that the volume is part
of a series entitled *Quaestiones Disputatae*. He acknowledges that there
are many disputed questions regarding such issues as the institution
of the sacraments by Christ "which are only too readily avoided in

the theology of the schools. Consequently, problems are propounded [in Rahner's book] which really are problems and which, accordingly, have not yet found a generally accepted solution."[20]

Throughout his small book, Rahner touches on several major unresolved issues and offers his views as a possible solution. The main theme of his volume is twofold: the meaning of church and the meaning of sacraments. He states that "The two concepts are intended to throw light on one another in the course of the inquiry so that a deeper understanding of the Church may be gained by asking what the sacraments are, and greater comprehension of the sacraments, by reflecting on what the church is." He immediately adds: "In the mind of the faithful at large, and perhaps even for theologians, the connection between Church and sacraments is not very clear."[21]

Rahner's volume is a straight-forward presentation of disputed issues regarding the church as a sacrament and regarding the seven ritual sacraments. For many decades, the ordinary presentation of the ritual sacraments centered on four factors:

1. Who is the legitimate minister of a given ritual sacrament?
2. Who is eligible to receive a given ritual sacrament?
3. What is the basic "matter" in a given ritual sacrament?
4. What is the basic "form" in a given ritual sacrament?

In Rahner's volume, these four issues are not the basic focus. Rather, he begins by considering certain basic characteristics found in the treatises on sacraments: such as, *opus operatum*, the reviviscence of the sacraments, *sacramentum* and *res sacramenti*, the way the sacraments cause grace, the institution of the sacraments by Christ, and sacramental and personal piety. In each of these sections, Rahner again and again raises *quaestiones disputatae* and tries to resolve the unresolved issues.

The positions of both Semmelroth and Rahner can be used by those who are teaching courses on the sacraments. Both theologians state very clearly that the Church itself is the basic sacrament, and the connection of church as sacrament with the sacramental rituals cannot be clearly explained in one or two class periods. I would think that the sacramental relationship of the church itself as sacrament to the church's sacramental rituals would need about one fourth of the entire semester. One or two lectures on this inter-relationship or one or two class discussions on this inter-relationship are inadequate. A contemporary class on sacraments cannot begin with baptism and end with the anointing of the sick. The link between the church as the basic sacrament and the sacramental rituals needs to be made in a strong and far-reaching way.

Another theologian, Juan Luis Segundo, in his volume, *The Sacraments Today*, entitled his introduction in a daring way: *A New Crisis for the Sacraments?*[22] Segundo offers us a stark challenge, which those who are teaching sacraments also need to take into account. Segundo writes:

> The sacramental life of the Church has gone into decline at different points in church history. But the decline we are now witnessing has a distinctive feature that makes it not only new but unique. It has not been brought on by ignorance, indifference, or rebellion against the Church. Difficult as it may be to believe at first glance, it has been brought on by the Church itself.[23]

Segundo was in tune with many other Catholic theologians who saw serious misconceptions in the prevalent theology of the church. From the time of Johann Sebastian von Drey (1777-1853) and Johann Adam Möhler (1796-1838) down to the middle of the twentieth century there were many Catholic voices urging a rethinking of ecclesiology. Émile Mersch (1890-1940), Erich Przywara (1889-1972), Sebastian

Tromp (1889-1975) and Louis Bouyer (1913-2004) were pressing for a renewal of ecclesiology. Segundo's call for a renewed ecclesiology rests on these antecedents, but he also brings to the table the issue of cultural diversity and social disparity. Because these issues were not treated very well when Segundo was writing, he held that the anti-church movements were brought on by the Catholic Church itself.

Fifty years after Vatican II, we have been blessed with new insights on the church as the basic sacrament. Not all the issues which the above authors have explained in detail are thoroughly integrated into the theologies of the seven ritual sacraments. Nonetheless, the insights of the four theologians just mentioned cannot be put to one side or disregarded, since the documents of Vatican II also stress the issue that the church itself is a sacrament.

On the issue of the church as sacrament, there is a strong connection between the positions of Schillebeeckx, Semmelroth, Rahner, and Segundo, and the position regarding the church as a sacrament that is found in the documents of Vatican II. Consequently, part three of this chapter is intimately connected to parts one and two of this chapter.

III. The Church is the Basic Sacrament

During the past fifty years, many theological writings have examined the meaning of sacrament as used by the Vatican II bishops when they said that the church is a sacrament. Some theologians and scholars stated that the bishops at Vatican II did not mean that the church was a sacrament; rather, they argued that the bishops only wanted to say that the church is "like" a sacrament, since the church can be described in many ways as a sign of God's love.

In order to clarify this controversy, let us begin with a listing of the seven instances in which the documents of Vatican II use the phrase "the church is a sacrament." I will list both the Latin text and the English translation.[24]

Constitutio Dogmatica De Ecclesia:
Lumen Gentium

1) Chapter one, paragraph one:

> Cum autem Ecclesia sit in Christo veluti sacramentum seu signum et instrumentum intimae cum Deo unionis totiusque generis humani unitatis, naturam missionemque suam universalem, praecedentium Conciliorum argumento instans, pressius fidelibus suis et mundo universo declarare intendit.

> Since the Church, in Christ, is a sacrament—a sign and instrument, that is, of communion with God and of the unity of the entire human race—it here proposes, for the benefit of the faithful and of the entire world, to describe more clearly, and in the tradition laid down by earlier councils, its own nature and universal mission.

2) Chapter two, paragraph 9:

> Deus congregationem eorum qui in Iesum, salutis auctorem et unitatis pacisque principium, credentes aspiciunt, convocavit et constituit Ecclesiam, ut sit universis et singulis sacramentum visibile huius salutiferae unitatis.

> All those who in faith look towards Jesus, the author of salvation and the source of unity and peace, God has gathered together and established as the Church, that it may be for each and every one the visible sacrament of this saving unity.

3) Chapter seven, paragraph 48:

> Christus quidem exaltatus a terra omnes traxit ad seipsum (cf. Io. 12, 32 gr); resurgens ex mortuis (cf. Rom. 6, 9) Spiritum suum vivificantem in discipulos immisit et per eum Corpus suum quod est Ecclesia ut universale salutis sacramentum constituit.

> Christ, when he was lifted up from the earth, drew all humanity to himself (see Jn 12:32, Greek text). Rising from the dead (see Rom 6:9) he sent his life-giving Spirit upon his disciples and through him set up his body which is the church

as the universal sacrament of salvation.

Constitutio Pastoralis
de Ecclesia in Mundo Huius Temporis:
Gaudium et Spes

4) Chapter four, paragraph 45:

Omne vero bonum quod Populus Dei in suae peregrinatio-
nis terrestris tempore hominum familiae praebere potest, ex
hoc profluit quod Ecclesia est "universale sacramentum,"
mysterium amoris Dei erga hominem manifestans simul et
operans.

Every benefit the people of God can confer on humanity during its earthly pilgrimage is rooted in the church's being "the
universal sacrament of salvation," at once manifesting and
actualizing the mystery of God's love for humanity.

Note: In both the Latin text and the English text, after the phrase
"the universal sacrament of salvation," there is a footnote reference to
Lumen Gentium, chapter VII, number 48, which is cited above.

Constitutio de Sacra Liturgia:
Sacrosanctum Concilium

5) Chapter one, paragraph 5:

Nam de latere Christi in cruce dormientis ortum est totius
Ecclesiae mirabile sacramentum.

For it was from the side of Christ as he slept the sleep of
death upon the cross that there came forth the wondrous sacrament of the whole church.

Note: In both the Latin text and the English text, after the phrase
"the wondrous sacrament of the whole church," there is a footnote
reference to Augustine, *Enarratio in Ps.* CXXXVIII, 2. There is also a
reference to the second reading for Holy Saturday, which is found in
Roman Missal.

6) Chapter one, paragraph 26:

> Actiones liturgicae non sunt actiones privatae, sed celebrationes Ecclesiae, quae est "unitatis sacramentum," scilicet plebs sancta sub Episcopis adunata et ordinata.

> Liturgical services are not private functions but are celebrations of the church which is "the sacrament of unity," namely, the holy people united and organized under their bishops.

Note: In both the Latin text and the English text, after the phrase "the church which is the sacrament of unity," there is footnote reference to St. Cyprian, *De cath. eccl. unitate*, 7.

Decretum de Activitate Missionali Ecclesiae: *Ad Gentes Divinitus*

7) Chapter one, number 5:

> Deinde, cum semel, morte et resurrectione sua, complevisset in seipso mysteria salutis nostrae et renovationis universorum, Dominus omnem potestatem adeptus in caelo et in terra, priusquam assumeretur in caelum, Ecclesiam suam ut sacramentum salutis fundavit.

> Later, before he was assumed into heaven (see Acts 1, 11), after he had fulfilled in himself the mysteries of our salvation and the renewal of all things by his death and resurrection, the Lord, who had received all power in heaven and on earth (see Mt. 28:18), founded his church as the sacrament of salvation.

In the documents of Vatican II, the church is called a sacrament. Only in the first citation from *Lumen Gentium* do the bishops use the Latin term, *"veluti,"* thereby modifying the term sacrament. This single use of the term *veluti* has divided Catholic theologians in a strong way. A number of these theologians maintain that the bishops in the documents of Vatican II understood the church not as a sacrament in itself, but simply "similar to a sacrament" (*veluti sacramentum*).

The Latin term, *velut* (or at times *veluti*), has as its first meaning a direct attribution: namely, "even as," or "just as," or "like as." Both Cicero and Virgil used the term in this positive way. However, there are secondary ways in which the term *velut* was used, namely: "as," or "for instance," or "for example." At times, Cicero used the term *velut* in this secondary and exemplary way. Another secondary meaning of *velut* is found when one is introducing a comparison or a figurative description: namely, "as," or "like," or "as it were." At times, Virgil used the term *velut* in this way. Yet another secondary use of *velut* can be found when one is introducing a hypothetical or comparative clause, namely: "just as if," or "as if," or "as though." One can find this use of *velut* in Julius Caesar and in Ovid.[25]

Given these various meanings of the term *velut*, how can one read its use in the opening paragraph of *Lumen Gentium*? Likeswise, given the fact that "veluti sacramentum" occurs only once in the Vatican II documents, this single use can only be seen in an ambiguous way, for nowhere in the documents of Vatican II is there any attempt to clarify its meaning. The fact that it is not used in the other six assertions that the church is a sacrament indicates that the bishops clearly called the church a sacrament.

That the documents of Vatican II clearly presented the church as a sacrament was verified in the following way. In December 1965, the Second Vatican Council came to an end. Three months later, March 20-26, 1966, the University of Notre Dame hosted an International Theological Conference in order to explore the meaning of Vatican II. Many theologians who had worked with the bishops during the council were invited not only to attend the conference but also to deliver papers regarding aspects of the council. The university also invited some well-known Protestant and Jewish scholars and they too were called on for Protestant or Jewish responses. All of the presentations were then published by the University of Notre Dame Press under the title: *Vatican II: An Interfaith Appraisal.*[26]

In several of the presentations, the phrase, "The Church is a sacrament," came to the fore. In Charles Moeller's essay, "History of *Lumen Gentium's* Structure and Ideas," he explained that the bishops were re-thinking the meaning of the church as a mystery and sign. This re-thinking was based on the theology of the mystical body which had emerged around 1925 and became very popular with the encyclical *Mystici Corporis Christi* by Pius XII (1943). Moeller also stated that the rethinking of church was also based on the theology of sign which had emerged basically in Germany prior to the council. We have considered the material on Semmelroth and Rahner in an earlier part of this chapter. The rethinking was also based on the ecumenical currents within the framework of the World Council of Churches, which had also taken place prior to the council. Moeller formulates the meaning of the term sacrament when it was used in the documents of Vatican II in the following way: "The Church is both mystery and sacrament; she is, then, tied first of all to the primordial mystery – that of the Trinity."[27]

Gérard Philips, another theological peritus at the council, presented an essay in the same conference titled "The Church: Mystery and Sacrament."[28] Many of his ideas correlate to those of Moeller. Both of these scholars state very clearly and very carefully that the church is a sacrament, and that this is what the council precisely wanted to state.

In Carlo Colombo's presentation, "The Hierarchical Structure of the Church," he states the issue once again: "In order to understand Catholic doctrine it is necessary never to lose sight of the fundamental concept used by the Council to define the Church – *sacramentum salutis.*"[29]

Jorge Medina Estevez, Charles Moeller, Yves Congar, Thomas

Stransky, Christopher Butler, Henri de Lubac, and others entered into a question and answer form of presentation at this conference. Medina Estevez mentioned that the council did not use the phrase primordial sacrament – *Ursakrament*.[30] However, the council, he reminds us, did refer to the church as sacrament. Medina Estevez, who was a peritus at the council, went out of his way to state that the bishops did indeed call the church a sacrament.

The essays developed in this conference at the University of Notre Dame must be taken seriously. These scholars had helped put together the documents of Vatican II, consequently their understanding of the many theological situations the bishops faced has major validity. All of these scholars are in agreement that the documents of Vatican II clearly teach that the church is a sacrament.

In many ways, the conciliar bishops' frequent use of the term sacrament has opened the door for further discussion and debate on sacramentality. Fifty years after the council, there is still a continuing discussion on the meaning of the phrase, "church as sacrament." However, the position that the church is a foundational sacrament has been officially accepted by the leadership of the Catholic Church, which means that we today can incorporate the church as a foundational sacrament into our teaching on the sacramental life of the Catholic Church.

IV. Sacraments are the Work of the Holy Trinity

In the revised edition of the *Catechism of the Catholic Church*, Part Two is entitled "The Celebration of the Christian Mystery."[31] It is in this lengthy part of the *Catechism* that the authors present sacramental theology. Part Two is divided into two sections.

- Section One is entitled "The Sacramental Economy," §§1076-1209.

- Section Two is entitled "The Seven Sacraments of the Church" §§1210-1690.

In a very clear way, the authors of the *Catechism* state that the material in Section One offers a basic understanding for the material in Section Two. The authors write:

> It is therefore important first to explain this "sacramental dispensation" (chapter one). The nature and essential features of liturgical celebrations will then appear more clearly (chapter two).[32]

In my study of these two sections of the *Catechism of the Catholic Church*, I came to the conclusion that the material in Section One, "The Sacramental Economy," presents a theology of sacraments which is fundamentally different from the theology of sacraments presented in Section Two, "The Seven Sacraments of the Church." The following pages explain my conclusion.

An Analysis of Section One: "The Sacramental Economy"

Section One begins with a theme that has had a major place in the history of Catholic theology, namely: "The Liturgy – Work of the Holy Trinity." In other words, to understand sacramental theology, we must begin with the relationship of sacramental theology to Trinitarian theology.[33] In the writings of every major theologian, a theology of God governs and shapes all other aspects of theological endeavor.

The authors of the *Catechism* present the relationship of sacramental theology to God the Father (§§1077-1083), to Jesus Christ (§§1084-1090), and to the Holy Spirit (§§1091-1109). In these pages, there is a remarkable foundation of sacramental theology, namely "The Liturgy – Work of the Holy Trinity".

1. The title of paragraphs explaining the relationship of God the Father to the sacraments reads: "The Father – Source and Goal of the Liturgy."

In one-and-a-half pages, the role of God the Father is explained in some detail. In this brief section, I noticed that the term "blessing" was used over and over again.

In §1077, blessing is mentioned three times.

In §1078, blessing is mentioned three times.

In §1079, blessing is mentioned two times.

In §1080, blessing is mentioned four times.

In §1081, blessing is mentioned three times.

In §1082, blessing is mentioned three times.

In §1083, blessing is mentioned three times.

One can rightly state that in this multiple mention of blessing, God the Father's main sacramental action is blessing. In baptism, God the Father blesses us. In Confirmation, God the Father blesses us. In the Eucharist, God the Father blesses us; etc. In the celebration of each sacrament, the most important action of God the Father is blessing.

In this brief section of the *Catechism*, the term blessing appears twenty-one times. In eighteen of these times, "blessing" refers primarily to God the Father who is blessing his people. Only three times (once in §1078, once in 1081, and once in 1083) is the term blessing used as a responding blessing by the members of Christian community to the blessings that have comes from God the Father to their community.

Given the above, we can easily ask an important question, namely: where should sacramental theology begin? The answer in this section of the *Catechism* is clear; we should begin with the "liturgy as the work of the Holy Trinity." We should begin our understanding of the sacraments with God the Father, who is blessing us in all of the sacraments. In this section of the *Catechism*, it is the Father's blessing in the sacraments that constitutes the foundation for the theological understanding of each and every sacramental celebration. The fundamental essence of all sacramental life is the blessing of God the Father.

To understand the reality of a sacramental celebration, these pages of the *Catechism* do not begin with matter, form, minister, or receiver of the sacraments. Rather, sacramental life originates in the amazing blessing of God the Father. Consequently, the theological beginning of a presentation on the humanity of Jesus as sacrament, or on the church as sacrament, or on the seven sacraments is not and should not be what we do. Rather, in order to understand Jesus as sacrament, the church as sacrament, or the seven sacraments, we need to begin with what God is doing. As we have just seen, God the Father is blessing us in and through the humanity of Jesus, in and through the Holy Spirit, in and through the sacramentality of the church, and in and through the celebration of the individual sacraments. What God is doing, not what we are doing, is the foundation for any theological presentation on the theology of sacraments.

2. Christ's Work in the Liturgy

When the authors of the *Catechism* focus on the second person of the Blessed Trinity, they focus on the Logos made flesh. The Incarnate Logos, Jesus, works in a primary way in all sacramental and non-sacramental liturgies. In this section, there is no single word, such as blessing, which dominates. Rather, it is the verbal structures of Jesus' work that stand out.

> In §1084, we read: "Christ now acts through the sacraments he instituted to communicate his grace."
>
> In §1084, we read: "The action of Christ" ... "makes present efficaciously the effect that they signify."
>
> In §1085, we read: "In the liturgy of the Church, it is principally his own Paschal mystery that Christ signifies and makes present."

In §1085, we read: All that Christ did "cannot remain only in the past," and "all that Christ is participates in the divine eternity, and so transcends all times," and "The event of the Cross and Resurrection abides and draws everything toward life."

In §1087, we read: "The risen Christ, by giving the Holy Spirit to the apostles, entrusted to them his power of sanctifying.

In §1088, we read: "Christ is always present in his Church, especially in her liturgical celebrations," and "He is present in the Sacrifice of the Mass."

In §1088, we read: "He is present in the sacraments so that when anybody baptizes, it is really Christ himself who baptizes."

In §1088, we read: "He is present in his word since it is he himself who speaks when the holy Scriptures are read in the Church."

In §1088, we read: "He is present when the Church prays and sings."

In §1089, we read: The church "participates in the liturgy of heaven."

The second Person of the Holy Trinity, Jesus the Logos, is central to all liturgies including sacramental liturgies. In all liturgies, Jesus is the primary minister. Once again, we can ask where we begin when we study sacramental theology. The answer, as seen above, is in the blessing of God the Father and in the primary presence and action of the Word Incarnate.

3. The Holy Spirit and the Church in the Liturgy

In the *Catechism*, the work of the Father is presented in a page and a half. The work of the Incarnate Logos is presented in two pages. The work of the Holy Spirit is presented in four-and-a-half pages. The work of the Holy Spirit is multiple. What I have asked my students to do is go through all of these pages and underline the nouns and verbs which express the activity of the Holy Spirit in the liturgy. For example:

> In §1091, we read: "<u>teacher of the faith</u> of the people of God and <u>artisan</u> of God's masterpiece.
>
> In §1091, we read: "The Spirit <u>encounters us</u> in the response of faith which He has aroused in us."
>
> In §1092, we read: "The Spirit <u>prepares</u> the Church to encounter her Lord."
>
> In §1093, we read: "The Holy Spirit <u>fulfills</u> what was prefigured in the Old Covenant."
>
> In §1098, we read: "The grace of the Holy Spirit <u>seeks to awaken</u> faith, conversion of heart, and adherence to the Father's will."

The listing of what the Holy Spirit does continues through the next three pages. Again we see that the essence of sacramental life is not what we do or what the church does or what the ordained minister does. These actions are all secondary. The essence of sacramental life and its theological explanation lies in what God the Father is doing, what the Incarnate Logos is doing, and what the Holy Spirit is doing.

Sacramental theology, whether we are focusing on the humanity of Jesus as the foundational sacrament or on the church as a basic sacrament or on any and every sacramental ritual, begins with what God is doing. Sacramental theology does not begin with what we are doing, or what the church assembly is doing, or what ordained ministers are doing. This focus on the beginning and foundation of sacramental life offers us a new form of sacramental theology.

In this new Trinitarian form of sacramental theology, the four questions mentioned above are secondary:

1. Who is the legitimate minister of a given ritual sacrament?
2. Who is eligible to receive a given ritual sacrament?
3. What is the basic "matter" in a given ritual sacrament?

4. What is the basic "form" in a given ritual sacrament?

Prior to all four of these questions, we need to ask:

1. What is the Father doing?

2. What is the Incarnate Logos doing?

3. What is the Holy Spirit doing?

The issues of "who is the minister," "who is the recipient," "what is the basic matter," and "what is the basic form" are all responses and reactions to what Father, Son, and Spirit are doing. Sacramental theology is not centered on human response. Rather, its center is on the "Work of the Holy Trinity." Only when we come to understand what the Trinity is doing in the sacraments can we, the Church, ordained ministers, and recipients ask what we are to do as a response to God's blessing, care, loving, forgiving, etc. The immediate response is gratitude to God. We bless God who has first blessed us.

In the lengthy four-and-one-half pages which describe the role of the Holy Spirit in sacramental life, we see that the Holy Spirit offers us an abundance of actions in liturgical and sacramental life of the Church. Given this abundance, we can ask: where do we begin when we study sacramental theology? The answer, as seen above, is in the blessing of God the Father, in the primary presence of the Word Incarnate, and in the multiple actions and presence of the Holy Spirit in our sacramental and liturgical life.

This section of the *Catechism* states in an abundant way a powerful understanding of sacramental theology and its beginnings in the loving and creative action of Father, Son, and Holy Spirit. If someone asks where we should begin our teaching on the sacraments, the *Catechism* provides us with a Trinitarian beginning that is expressed in a powerful way.

However, the *Catechism* offers another quite different presentation on sacramental theology (Part Two, Section Two), which is based on a totally different sacramental dispensation. In other words, Section One deals with the sacramental economy, but the explanation presented in Section One is not used in Section Two when it deals with the seven sacraments of the church.

4. The Sacramental Celebration of the Paschal Mystery

Chapter Two of Section One is entitled "The Sacramental Celebration of the Paschal Mystery." In this part of the *Catechism*, the authors focus on the actual celebration of the Church's Liturgy (§§1135-1209). To do this, the authors pose four questions whose answers describe the meaning and depth of sacramental liturgy. The four questions are the following.

1. Who celebrates the liturgy?
2. How is the liturgy celebrated?
3. When is the liturgy celebrated?
4. Where is the liturgy celebrated?

Let us consider each of these questions and explore the main answers that the *Catechism* gives to each of these questions.

a. The first question, "Who celebrates the liturgy?" is answered in the following way:

- "Liturgy is an 'action' of the *whole Christ* (*Christus totus*)" (§1136).
- "It is the whole community, the Body of Christ united with its Head that celebrates"[34] (§1140).
- "Not all members have the same function. In the celebration of the liturgy there are ordained and non-ordained ministers, but their ministries are at the service of the people of God and more fundamentally at the service of Christ the High Priest" (§§1142-1144).

b. The second question, "How is the Liturgy Celebrated?" is answered in the following way:

- There are multiple answers to how the liturgy is celebrated. The many ways in which the liturgy is celebrated are mentioned in paragraphs 1145-1162. In these paragraphs, the authors of the *Catechism* indicate that liturgy is celebrated through an abundance of signs and symbols (§§1145 – 1152). Liturgy is also celebrated through an abundance of words and actions (§§1153 – 1155), through singing and music (§§1156 – 1158), and finally, through the veneration of holy images (§§1159 – 1162).

- It is obvious that the celebration of liturgy is not confined to matter, form, minister, and the person ministered to. Rather, liturgy reveals the presence of God the Father, who blesses us through an abundance of signs and symbols, through an abundance of words and actions, through singing and music, and through holy images.

c. The third question, "When is the Liturgy Celebrated?" is answered in the following way:

- In §§1163 – 1178, we read that these times are multiple: liturgical seasons, the Lord's Day, the liturgical year, the celebration of the feasts of saints, and the liturgy of the hours.

d. The fourth question, "Where is the Liturgy Celebrated?" is answered in the following way:

- In §§1179 – 1186, we read: "The worship 'in Spirit and truth' of the New Covenant is not tied exclusively to any one place. The whole earth is sacred and entrusted to the children of men. What matters above all is that, when the faithful assemble in the same place, they are the 'living stones,' gathered to be 'built into a spiritual house.'"

There is an openness to liturgy in all four answers which helps us understand the basic issue of the liturgy. Through the who, how, when and where questions, we see that the Holy Trinity is at work in all of these areas, and that the *Christus totus* is also celebrating in the abundance of the who, how, when and where dimensions of liturgy.

The final pages of Section One focus on liturgical diversity and the unity of mystery. In §1200, we read: "The mystery of Christ is so unfathomably rich that it cannot be exhausted by its expression in any single liturgical tradition." We also read in §1202 that "the diverse liturgical traditions have arisen by the very reason of the Church's mission. Churches of the same geographical and cultural area came to celebrate the mystery of Christ through particular expressions characterized by the culture: in the tradition of the 'deposit of faith,' in liturgical symbolism, in the organization of fraternal communion, in the theological understanding of the mysteries, and in various forms of holiness." In these paragraphs, there is an openness—within boundaries—for cultural diversification.

In the *Catechism*, the sacramental theology of Section One is meant to be foundational. In this section we can perceive many of the issues on ecclesiology which had arisen from 1900 through Vatican II and even down to today. These issues include an ecclesiology which has its origin in the work of the Trinitarian God; an ecclesiology in which Jesus is central both as originator and as minister; an ecclesiology in which multi-cultural aspects are honored; an ecclesiology in which the sacraments are celebrated by the whole community; and an ecclesiology which is open to Christian ecumenism and even, at least in a beginning way, to non-Christian religions.

What is expressed in Section One regarding sacramental theology is not the same as what was expressed in the presentations on the sacraments which were stated in the pre-Vatican II theological textbooks. However, none of this new approach would have happened if the bishops at Vatican II had not expressed these positions in their most important document, *Lumen Gentium*. In other words, the authors of this first section of the *Catechism* wanted this material to be the base on which the Second Section would build its theology of the seven sacraments.

The *Catechism of the Catholic Church* begins its presentation on the church by citing the opening paragraph of *Lumen Gentium*.

> Christ is the light of humanity; and it is, accordingly, the heart-felt desire of this sacred Council, being gathered together in the Holy Spirit, that, by proclaiming his Gospel to every creature, it may bring all men that light of Christ which shines out visible from the Church (§748).

The authors of the *Catechism* then add their own explanation:

> By choosing this starting point, the Council demonstrates that the article of faith about the Church depends entirely on the articles concerning Christ Jesus. The Church has no other light than Christ's; according to a favorite image of the Church Father, the Church is like the moon, all its light reflected from the sun (§748).

To explain this core of Christian life, Bonaventure Kloppenburg uses the phrase, "The Church as mystery of the moon." Kloppenburg was a peritus at Vatican II, and so his analysis of *Lumen Gentium* has a strong foundation. He bases his position on the Dogmatic Constitution on the Church, *Lumen Gentium*, promulgated by the bishops at Vatican II.

> The Council begins its Dogmatic Constitution on the Church with the words, *Lumen Gentium*. But this "light of the nations" is not the Church: "Christ is the light of all nations"! (LG 1/14). From its very opening words, therefore, Vatican II seeks to give a completely Christocentric and thus relativized idea of the Church. We can understand the Church only if we relate it to Christ, the glorified Lord.[35]

Kloppenburg goes on to say that whenever the church itself is absolutized, separated from Christ and considered only in its structures, it ceases to be a mystery and becomes simply another religious society or organization. It ceases to deserve special attention. He continues:

> Only Christ is the light of the world. He is the Sun, sole source of light. At the side of the Sun, which is Christ, stands the Church like the moon which receives all its light, brilliance and warmth from the sun.[36]

Kloppenburg continues this imagery. He writes that Christian communities have a borrowed light which waxes and wanes. The light of the Christian communities is no more than a "pale shimmer" or a "dark radiance." Christian communities' witnessing to God can often become obscured. Even though the Christian communities have been called "salt of the earth," they can become tasteless. Even more, Christian communities can be excessively human. Only when they draw intimately near to Christ do they reflect the Sun. The human Jesus, however, reflects God. Ultimately, then, God is the unending sunlight, reflected in and through Jesus and from Jesus into the Christian communities. It is the light of God that draws people to Jesus and to the Christian community. However, the reflection of God in both the human Jesus and in the Christian communities is limited. We can catch only a glimpse or glimmer of God who is infinite light. The divine light goes beyond all boundaries and has no limits whatsoever.

In the above paragraphs, we can catch only a small glimpse of the spiritual beauty of the Christian religion. Ultimately, the spiritual beauty is the transcendent God and the Christian communities share in that beauty when, like the moon which has no light of its own, they reflect the human Jesus who is the Light of the World (*Lumen Gentium*) and they reflect his humanity, which is the sacrament of God.[37]

It is probably clear to the readers that I am very accepting of the sacramental theology as found in Section One of the *Catechism*. This section of the *Catechism*, as mentioned above, expresses much of the theology on Church and on Jesus as developed from 1900 to the present.

V. The Seven Sacraments of the Church

As we focus on the *Catechism's* second section on the sacraments, namely on the seven sacraments of the Church, we should recall the opening introductory passage which appears prior to both Section One and Section Two:

> It is therefore important first to explain this "sacramental dispensation" (chapter one). The nature and essential features of liturgical celebrations will then appear more clearly (§1076).

There are number of issues in Section Two, "The Seven Sacraments of the Church," that make me hesitant about its theology of the sacraments. The first issue is the lack of inter-connection with Section One. The introductory material in Section One is supposed to offer a basic understanding of the material in Section Two as the above citation states very clearly. However, in the opening paragraphs of Section Two, there is no reference to the material in Section One. The authors do not state that the material in Section Two is meant to elaborate on the sacramental dispensation as explained in Section One. The lack of such an inter-connection indicates that the authors of chapter are not using the sacramental dispensation. Rather, Section Two begins by stating that "Christ instituted the seven sacraments of the new law." This is followed by a brief listing and explanation for each of the seven sacraments (§§1210-1211).

I have read Section One, which was explained in part four of this chapter, many times, and I have appreciated its insights in a very strong way. In my view, Section One contains a powerful way of beginning lectures and writings on sacramental life, namely: "The Liturgy – Work of the Holy Trinity." The work of the Trinity offers an excellent foundation for all other sacramental discussion today. It is my judgment that there was one committee who wrote Section One and a quite different committee who wrote Section Two. I am unable to prove this, but the two sections, theologically and liturgically, are widely distinct and different.

I have also read the material in Section Two over and over. I have concluded that the pages in the *Catechism* on the seven sacraments of the church, namely Section Two, are in many ways almost a re-run of the sacramental theology one finds in the Catholic theological textbooks from 1800 to 1950. Structurally, the authors begin their presentations of the individual sacraments in the same way. Moreover, in the presentation of each of the seven sacraments, the standard pre-Vatican II format was used, namely: (a) the naming of this sacrament based on New Testament and early church writings; (b) the institution of the seven sacraments by Jesus; (c) the basic liturgical structure of each sacrament which has never changed; (d) the minister of the sacrament; (e) the one who can receive a given sacrament; (f) and the matter and form of each sacrament. It seems that the overreaching tendency of Section Two is to re-state the usual doctrine of the sacraments.

Another issue, which is not present in Section Two, is the minimal use of the history of the seven sacraments. On a few occasions, the authors do refer to some historical details, but for the most part the authors do not show that they have incorporated the one-hundred-and-twenty-years of historical research on each of the seven sacraments. From 1896 down to 2013, scholars have laboriously researched the history of each sacrament and this historical material has called into question many major pre-suppositions of the Neo-Scholastic approach to sacraments. Since the authors of Section Two are minimalistic in their references to this sacramental history, their presentations of the seven sacraments are questionable. This caveat will become clearer as we consider the seven presentations of Catholic sacramental life.

In a brief way, let us consider the manner in which each of themes is presented by the authors of Section Two. The authors begin each section with the various names of each sacrament.

1. The Naming of Baptism, the Sacrament of Initiation

The opening title of the section on baptism reads: "What is this sacrament called?" The authors present a listing of names: "baptism," the "sacrament of initiation," the "washing of regeneration and renewal by the Holy Spirit," and "enlightenment" (§§1214-1216). The person who is baptized is called "the son or daughter of light," for he or she has become "light." There is a connection between the baptism of a man or woman, and the baptism of Christ (§§1223-1224). The one who is baptized puts on Christ, who lived and died for all of us.

When did Jesus institute baptism as a sacrament? In the history of sacramental theology, we find a much divided view:

- St. Thomas writes that this institution of baptism as a sacrament took place at Jesus' own baptism.

- It was begun on the occasion of Nicodemus' visit to Jesus. This was proposed by Estius, but Lercher noted that this opinion was somewhat unique.

- John Duns Scotus and Francisco de Suárez selected an occasion after Jesus' baptism, but before he met with Nicodemus.

- Aphrates, who died around 345, had suggested that Jesus instituted all seven sacraments at the Last Supper.

- Finally, Alexander of Hales and Melchior Cano proposed a time around the Ascension when Jesus sent out his disciples.

From the time of the Ascension to about the fourth century, it seems that only adults were baptized. In the early Jesus-communities, it was not, generally speaking, the custom to baptize infants.[38] The time of the catechumenate was a time of spirituality and not an academic introduction to the Christian faith. The catechumens came together, prayed together, and heard from a Catechist who Jesus was and what Jesus did. The Catechists were lay men and women. The custom of a time of spiritual growth and baptismal washings was common to many parts of the Jewish people at the time Jesus. The Essenes had a form of baptismal washing before the celebration of a Jewish prayer. Many religious sects also had similar religious washings. Basically, the focus was on spirituality rather than on an intellectual understanding of the given religion.[39]

At the end of a prayer-session with the catechumens, the lay person led them in prayer and in a few places the lay person laid his or her hands on the head of each catechumen, asking the Holy Spirit to come and bless the person. More often than not, the catechumenate lasted about a year. In many ways, we have today a similar form of the catechumenate, namely the RCIA, which is meant to be a time of spirituality, but too often it has become a time of academic lecturing. At the conclusion of the catechumenate, each catechumen is baptized, confirmed and receives the Eucharist.

We can learn much from the RCIA, for we can see the close interweaving of baptism to confirmation and both of these sacraments interwoven with the Eucharist. The goal of the entire RCIA is an entry into the Christian community through these three inter-woven sacraments. The *Catechism* states: "In the Roman liturgy the post-baptismal anointing announces a second anointing with sacred chrism to be conferred later by the bishop – Confirmation which will as it were 'confirm' and complete the baptismal anointing" (§1242).

I would prefer to say that in the RCIA Baptism-Confirmation is really a single sacrament leading to the Eucharist. About twenty years ago, the Roman Curia allowed priests to baptize and confirm a young six or seven-year-old. Again there is one ceremony, baptism-confirmation. Even in the 300s and 400s when baptism and confirmation were separated, there was a union between baptism-confirmation.

This early century separation took place because the catechumen is not simply entering into a small parish church community. Rather, the catechumen is entering into a larger church community, namely the diocese. The bishops then made the rounds of the village churches and in a major sense "completed" the baptismal process. With the interval between the village church baptism and the visit of the bishop became more and more extensive, then theologians gradually developed a "theology of confirmation," which basically centered on a more mature "completion" of the catechumen's entry into the Catholic world. With an interval of seven, ten, even fifteen years, the theological explanation of the linkage of baptism and confirmation became more and more separate. We can learn more about the meaning of baptism-confirmation in and through the RCIA and baptism-confirmation for young children. We can also learn much from the Eastern Churches, many of which baptize and confirm babies. The more distance we place between baptism and confirmation, the less understanding we will have regarding the union between baptism-confirmation.

In the *Catechism*, the issue of the necessity of baptism is studied (§§1257-1261). In this section, original sin is not mentioned by name, but it seems that it is at least implicit in §1257, in which the salvation of unbaptized infants is center-stage. In § 1263, the authors do mention original sin. It is interesting to note that in the latest ritual for the baptism of infants, the term original sin is mentioned only once, and this single mention occurs in the prayer of exorcism. To some degree, the new ritual for infant baptism does not emphasize original sin which used to be the centering point of infant baptism.

A highlight in the section on baptism can be found in §1266, in which we hear:

> "The Holy Trinity gives the baptized sanctifying grace...
>
> enabling them to believe in God, to hope in him, and to love him...
>
> gives them the power to live and act under the prompting of the Holy Spirit ...
>
> and allows them to grow in goodness through the moral virtues."

This small paragraph is strongly connected to Section One in which we have eight pages on sacramental liturgy as the Work of the Holy Trinity.[40] However, the structure of this entire chapter on baptism in Section Two is formed in the following way:

1. The naming of the sacrament of baptism;
2. Baptism and the economy of salvation;
3. Christ's baptism and it connection to the Church's baptism;
4. The ritual celebration and meaning of baptism and its mystagogy;
5. Who can receive baptism?
6. Who can baptize?
7. Is baptism necessary?
8. The spiritual effects of baptism.

A major pre-Vatican II textbook on sacramental theology, *Sacrae*

Theologiae Summa, was published in 1962, the same year in which Vatican II began. The author on the sacrament of baptism, Francisco Solá, divided his section on the sacrament of baptism as follows:

1. The naming of the sacrament of baptism;
2. The institution of baptism in the Christian economy of salvation;
3. The essence of the sacrament of baptism;
4. Is baptism necessary?
5. Who can receive baptism?
6. Who can baptize?
7. The spiritual effects of baptism.

The format of these two explanations on baptism is very similar. Solá's explanation is pre-Vatican II, and the explanation in the *Catechism* is post-Vatican II but resembles pre-Vatican II theology of baptism.

However, there are other ways to begin a study of sacraments. One might begin with the history of a given sacrament in the Western church. This has some good points, since it highlights what historical issues can truly be traced from apostolic times onward, and which historical issues have caused changes in the celebration and even in the theology of a given sacrament.

Another format that can be used as a starting point is Jesus in his human nature as the foundational sacrament. We have seen this in Schillebeeckx's writings, for he starts with Jesus as the foundational sacrament. We also saw this in the writings of Semmelroth and Rahner, both of whom see the church as the fundamental and foundational sacrament. We can also see this in the documents of Vatican II in which the bishops assert that the church is a foundational sacrament, and that Jesus is *Lumen Gentium*. In the Vatican II documents, Jesus as *Lu-*

men Gentium is explained in a fairly sacramental way: Jesus in his human nature reflects God, and Jesus in his humanity reflects God to us. Sacraments are always a sacrament of something and a sacrament to someone. In his humanity, Jesus reflects the love of God (of something) to all human beings (to someone). We may not call Jesus a foundational sacrament, but when the focus of the bishops at Vatican II is on Jesus who is the *Lumen Gentium*, there are sacramental overtones.

Still another format for sacramental theology is found in the section of the *Catechism* which in Section One is entitled: "Sacramental Liturgy – the Work of the Holy Trinity." In chapter four, I will attempt to explain this starting point in a more detailed way.

In Section Two on the sacraments, the authors have in strong measure retained the format of a theology of sacraments which one can call pre-Vatican II or Neo-Scholastic. It is precisely this issue which cautions me against advocating the use of Section Two in a class on sacramental theology. The material in this section of the *Catechism* seems to be somewhat outdated.

2. The Sacrament of Confirmation, a Sacrament of Initiation

The title of this section in the *Catechism* is "Confirmation in the economy of salvation." Confirmation is also presented as "the outpouring of the Holy Spirit," "the laying on of hands," and an "anointing with holy oil" (§§1286 – 1321). In §1290, the text states: "In the first centuries, confirmation generally comprised one single celebration with baptism." The authors then describe the differences between the Western and Eastern Churches, and they go so far as to say: "The practice of the Eastern Churches gives greater emphasis to the unity of Christian initiation" (§1292). Both the RCIA and the baptism-confirmation of children of catechetical age also give greater emphasis to the unity of baptism-confirmation.

There is a difficulty inherent in the way that the authors of this section describe the sacrament of confirmation. The authors, it seems, struggle to provide a theology of the separated sacrament of confirmation (§§1297-1301). In these paragraphs, the authors are prolonging the theology of the sacrament of confirmation which is not connected to baptismal theology. In my view, a better emphasis would be the construction of a theology of the sacrament of confirmation in and through its intimate connection with the sacrament of baptism. Then, one could emphasize the way in which the RCIA liturgy has radically changed confirmation from a "sacrament by itself" to a "co-sharing with the sacrament of initiation, baptism and confirmation." The same radical change can be seen in the baptism of children who have reached a catechetical age and are eligible for baptism-confirmation.

In the years after Vatican II, the age of confirmation was often determined by the bishop of a local diocese. One example indicates this problem of age for confirmation. The bishops of two adjacent dioceses in California, namely the diocese of Sacramento and the diocese of Oakland, worked in opposite directions. The bishop of Sacramento urged the parishes to schedule confirmation for young children of catechetical age. The bishop of Oakland took an opposite direction, for he advised his pastors to arrange for confirmation when the young men and women were in their final teen years. The Sacramento River separated these two dioceses, but the regulations for confirmation separated them even further. At the edges of the diocese, some families lived in one diocese but their children went to Catholic schools on the other side of the dividing river. Their bishop stresses either a younger or an older age for confirmation, while the school urged the opposite.

Theologians can do much for the sacrament of confirmation. They can emphasize the unity between baptism and confirmation. When theologians attempt to give a theological understanding of confirmation as a separate sacrament from baptism, they are not truly using the scriptural passages for baptism-confirmation or the statements of early church writers in a correct way. Such theologians are trying to place a special sacramental meaning on biblical and early church passages that were not present when they were written. Hopefully the leaders of the church, both institutional such as bishops and priests as well as leaders who are teaching theology, will work together to bring baptism and confirmation into some sort of unified theological understanding.

3. The Sacrament of the Eucharist, a Sacrament of Initiation

The title of this section of the Catechism is "'The Eucharist is Source and Summit of Ecclesial Life," but in the material that follows, the Eucharist is also called "Thanksgiving to God," "Breaking of Bread," "Eucharistic Assembly," "Memorial of the Lord's Passion and Resurrection," "the Holy Sacrifice," the "Holy and Divine Liturgy," "Holy Communion," and "Holy Mass" (§§1322-1419).

In the *Catechism*, this section on the Eucharist is the longest section dedicated to any individual sacrament, consisting of twenty-three pages. However, the length is necessary since the Eucharist is extremely central to the Christian Church. Over the centuries, there have been many attempts to clarify and even systematize a theology of Eucharist.

After expressing a few major titles for the Eucharist, the authors begin a major section of the Eucharist focusing on the economy of salvation (§§1333-1344). This is followed by a second very important section of Eucharistic theology, namely, the sacramental celebration of the Eucharist (§§1345-1327). A third section focuses on three major and fairly difficult aspects of the Eucharist, namely, the Eucharist as sacrifice, the Eucharist as thanksgiving, and thirdly the Eucharist as a memorial (§§1356-1381). In the final two sections (§§1382-1405), the authors center on the Eucharist as the paschal banquet and as the pledge of the glory to come.

Each of these sections is deeply important to Eucharistic theology. However, one could also use a very different format, beginning with the sacramental liturgy, including the Eucharist as the work of the Holy Trinity, which would connect the pages of Section Two to the pages of Section One. In the explanation of the Eucharist, as formulated by the authors of Section Two especially in §1376, the authors show us how strongly this theology of Eucharist is indebted to an Aristotelian form of theology. "The heart of the Eucharistic celebration," the authors tell us, "is the bread and wine that, by the words of Christ and the invocation of the Holy Spirit become Christ's body and blood." In the Glossary of the *Catechism*, we find a theological description of this change, which is called "transubstantiation."

> Transubstantiation: The scholastic term used to designate the unique change of the Eucharistic bread and wine into the Body and Blood of Christ. "Transubstantiation" indicates that through the consecration of the bread and wine there occurs a change of the entire substance of bread into the substance of the Body of Christ, and of the entire substance of the wine into the blood of Christ – even though the appearances of "species" of bread and wine remain.[41]

The understanding of the Eucharist in this analysis is based entirely on Aristotle's presentation of substance. The paragraph in the Glossary makes a direct reference to the text in §1376, in which the authors cite the wording of the Council of Trent. The authors of the *Catechism* do not make any reference to the efforts by contemporary Catholic theologians who use the terms trans-signification or transfinalization rather than transubstantiation.[42] Since Vatican II, some Catholic theologians have been attempting to move beyond Aristotelian boundaries.

In the text, we also read that "the Eucharistic presence of Jesus begins at the moment of the consecration and endures as long as the Eucharistic species subsist" (§1376). Once again, the Aristotelian language takes over with the term subsists. This wording, from Aristotelian philosophy, signifies the form by which there is a change, while the bread and wine signify the matter of the sacrament, the essence of which is also changed. Catholics, for many years, have allowed a philosophy to dictate the understanding of their belief.

In today's post-Vatican II church, what if someone attempted to explain the Eucharist in a philosophy other than Aristotelian? Let us imagine the use of Asian philosophies, instead of Greek philosophy. Clearly, the Church leadership has urged Catholic to move into other cultural expression of the Christian Church. Can we employ Asian philosophies or African philosophies to explain the theology of sacraments, especially the Eucharistic sacrament? At the moment, this is only a question, but it is certainly an essential part of allowing other cultures to help form our expression of Christian faith.

As the reader may also notice, there is no allusion to "The Sacramental Liturgy – the Work of the Holy Trinity." Even though this theme was described in many pages of Section One, it was not picked up by the authors of Section Two.[43] In paragraph 1360, there is a small and marginal reference to the blessings of God the Father. Paragraph 1360 reads:

> The Eucharist is a sacrifice of thanksgiving to the Father, a blessing by which the Church expresses her gratitude to God for all his benefits, for all that he has accomplished through creation, redemption, and sanctification. Eucharist means

first of all "thanksgiving."

There is a weak connection between this paragraph and the fairly lengthy paragraph in Section One, §1083. In Section One the main emphasis was on the work of Trinity, with the Father as the source and goal of liturgy. We have seen above in Section One the many times that the world blessing is used in a page and a half. For almost all of the blessings, the emphasis was on God the Father blessing us. It would be a great step forward if we showed that in every sacramental ceremony the most important thing is God blessing us. In the final paragraph, §1083, the text indicates that we Christians need to bless God, but it does not say that our blessing of God is a response to the unceasing blessing of us by God the Father. In sacramental liturgy God is blessing us again and again. It is the lack of mention of the Work of the Trinity in Section Two that contributes to the immense divide between Section One and Section Two.

In Section Two, there are two times that a paragraph has referenced the question: "Who celebrates the Eucharist?" These are found in §§1136 and 1140. In Section Two, §1348 and §1382 refer to the issue of who celebrates the Eucharist. The authors clearly state that liturgy is celebrated by the whole community. This means that Jesus is "the principal agent of the Eucharist." "The bishop or priest is acting in the person of Christ the head. He 'presides over the assembly'; he 'speaks after the readings'; 'he receives the offerings' of bread and wine; and 'he says the Eucharistic Prayer." "Others have their own parts to play: readers, those who bring up the offerings, those who give out communion, and the whole people whose "Amen" manifests their participation."

Somehow this lengthy citation does not have the depth of Section One in which we read: "Who celebrates? Liturgy is an action of the *whole Christ (Christus Totus)"* (§1136). "It is the whole community, the Body of Christ united with its Head that celebrates" (§1140). Given these words of Section One, we might expect a greater openness to the participation of the lay Christians. Merely saying "amen" is hardly a major ministry. "It is the whole community, the Body of Christ united with its Head, which celebrates." These issues from Section One are major factors as regards sacramental liturgy, and the authors of Section One cited an important quotation from *Sacrosanctum Concilium*:

> Liturgical services are not private functions but are celebrations of the Church which is "the sacrament of unity: namely the holy people united and organized under the authority of the bishops. Therefore, liturgical services pertain to the whole Body of the Church. They manifest it, and have effect upon it. But they touch individual members of the Church in different ways, depending on their order, their role in the liturgical services, and their actual participation in them (SC 28).

The authors of Section Two of the *Catechism* do not seem to base their work on the preceding section, and yet the preceding section was meant to be a basis for Section Two and its explanation of the seven sacraments.

4. The Sacrament of Penance, a Sacrament of Healing

The title of this section of the *Catechism* is "The Sacrament of Penance and Reconciliation." There are other descriptive names which are used for this sacrament as well: "Sacrament of Conversion," "Sacrament of Penance," "Sacrament of Confession," "Sacrament of Forgiveness," and "Sacrament of Reconciliation." (§§1423-1449).

The history of this sacrament has been studied for over one hundred years. Only a little of this history has had an influence on the text in the *Catechism*, which deals with the sacrament of reconciliation. However, we do find references to this historical data in §§1434-1470.[44]

For instance, the authors take it for granted that Jesus instituted the sacrament of reconciliation. However, they admit that over the centuries, the concrete form of this sacrament in which the Church has exercised this power received from the Lord has varied considerably. They then add: "During the first centuries the reconciliation of Christians who had committed particularly grave sins after their Baptism (for example, idolatry, murder, or adultery) was tied to a very rigorous discipline, according to which penitents had to do public penance for their sins, often for a year before receiving reconciliation" (§1447). This generalized statement is descriptive of the situation, but implications of the facts which are alluded to in the citation raise questions as to Jesus' institution of the sacrament. Nowhere in the gospels do we read that "the sacrament of reconciliation is limited to three major sins."

In the post-apostolic period, Hermas (c. 140) is one of the first writers who provides us with identifiable references to a specific ritualized practice of reconciliation. However, the best we can say about the writing of Hermas is this: After baptism there is but one and once only possibility for reconciliation to the church and this reconciliation is ecclesial and has a public quality about it.[45] Nowhere in the gospels does Jesus speak about a once-only reconciliation.

A second early verification of a ritual of reconciliation can be found in Tertullian (150-230). In his pre-Montanist writings, Tertullian clearly states that there is some ritualistic form of reconciliation for serious sin after baptism. Tertullian does not describe the ritual, but in his Montanist writings he does allude to a reconciliation ritual. However, it may not have been open for all sinners.

Clement of Alexandria (c. 215) refers to reconciliation for post-baptismal sins, but he does not describe the ritual. Origen (c. 253) allows post-baptismal forgiveness and lists many ways in which this forgiveness is attained: martyrdom, almsgiving, charity, fraternal forgiveness and—he includes—"hard and laborious remission of sin through penance." Down to the Council of Nicaea and beyond, the three capital sins of apostasy, adultery, and murder continued to be seen as unforgiveable. During the persecution in North Africa, when Cyprian was bishop of Carthage, he went back and forth over the sinfulness and the possibility of forgiveness for those who had denied their faith. At a council in Carthage in 251, it was decided that those who were *libellatici* (they had only written that they gave up their faith) could be reassumed into the church after adequate penance. The *sacrificati*, those who had offered sacrifices to the Roman Gods, and the *thurificati*, who had placed incense before the Roman Gods, could not be forgiven until they were at the moment of death. None of this is found in the gospels.

This historical material on the forgiveness of sin in the Catholic Church clearly indicates that there is no ritual of forgiveness which can be traced back to Jesus and the apostles. Rather, the issue of sin, especially the three major sins mentioned above, left the Catholic community with no means of forgiveness for those who committed such sins. Therefore, we have to say that the ritualized sacrament of reconciliation did not appear until the third century and even then it did not cover all sins.

In time, a ritual of reconciliation of major sins did become standard in the Western Catholic Church, but it was a form of reconciliation which was open only once in a person's lifetime. The Celtic Church did not focus on either no reconciliation at all or a single reconciliation during one's life. The Celtic Church developed the form we have today; namely, that Catholics can receive the sacrament of reconciliation as often as they wish. However, the history of how the Celtic Church form of reconciliation became standard for the Western Catholic Church is a long history in which many major Catholic leaders condemned the Celtic form. It is a long history, from the sixth century down to the thirteenth century. Even then, when personal and private confession finally became the common form of the sacrament of reconciliation, it was not officially endorsed. Only at the Council of Trent do we find an official acceptance of frequent confession. The bishops at Trent established the law of the church which required those who had committed serious sin to confess once a year.

In the *Catechism*, a few references to this history do appear (especially §1447), but the authors do not develop any conclusion from this history. They simply continue to assert that the sacrament of reconciliation goes back to Jesus and the apostles, and they make no mention that for the first 900 years of Christian existence most Christians never received this sacrament at all. The form of reconciliation which we have today is a form that the Celtic Church brought into the Catholic Church, but it was not really until the end of the 12th century that the Roman form of reconciliation was no longer in practice. In those early centuries, many Catholics never went to confession during their whole life. Does this non-reception of the sacrament have any ramifications for a theology of reconciliation today? Is our present form of the sacrament of penance of pastoral value? The *Catechism* offers no answer to these questions.

Once again, what I see in Section Two of the *Catechism* is a restatement of pre-Vatican II theology of the sacrament of penance. There is adequate historical data to this theology of the sacrament, but the authors of the *Catechism* evidently did not want to touch on the issue since the historical material raises substantial questions for Neo-Scholastic theology.

5. The Sacrament of the Anointing of the Sick, a Sacrament of

Healing

The title of this section of the *Catechism* is "The Anointing of the Sick." The presentation of this sacrament begins with a short explanation of illness and suffering which sets the stage for "Christ the Physician." In the New Testament, Jesus cures people who are sick. There is no doubt that Jesus in the gospels is a healer.

Taking care of the sick has been a part of gospel living from the early centuries onward. In almost all the civilized sections of the world at the time of Jesus, an anointing with oil was often used for medical purposes. The sacrament of the anointing of the sick has often been referred to as "A Sacrament for the Sick," "The Sacred Anointing of the Sick," and in the early middle ages as "Extreme Unction" (§§1499-1532).

In the *Catechism*, the eight pages on the anointing of the sick are presented under five headings:

1. Its Foundation in the Economy of Salvation.
2. Who Receives and Who Administers the Sacrament?
3. How is This Sacrament Celebrated?
4. The Effect of the Celebration of This Sacrament.
5. Viaticum, the Last Sacrament of the Christian.

The authors of the *Catechism* use a standard Neo-Scholastic outline when they present the material on the sacrament of the anointing of the sick. In the *Sacrae Theologiae Summa*, Francisco Solá used the following but similar outline:

1. The existence of Extreme Unction;
2. The essence of Extreme Unction;
3. The effects of Extreme Unction;
4. The subject and minister of Extreme Unction;
5. The necessity, the repetition, and the revival of Extreme Unc-

tion.

One of the major differences between the description of the anointing of the sick in the *Catechism* and the usual form of presenting this sacrament in the Neo-Scholastic approach is the change of names. From the thirteenth century down to contemporary times, this sacrament began to be called Extreme Unction, since it was a sacrament for those close to death. In the middle of the twentieth century onward, the use of this sacrament was extended to Christians who were seriously sick but not necessarily close to dying.

The authors of the *Catechism* explain the situation of illness and Christian life in their opening section, which describes the foundation of a sacrament of healing in the economy of salvation. Over the centuries of human life, illness and suffering have been "among the gravest problems" confronting human life (§1500). Illnesses often provide a person with a glimpse of death, and often do lead to personal anguish, self-centeredness, and even despair. On the other hand, a time of illness can also help a Christian turn to God in a closer way. In the Old Testament and in the New Testament, mention is made that human illness and human sin go together. The fall of Adam and Eve brought about a life that is frail and open to sickness.

Some of the most moving sections of the gospels center on Jesus the healer, and this image of Jesus healing the sick has encouraged Christian communities from earliest times onward to reach out and help those who are sick. The authors of the *Catechism* present a major statement of the Council of Trent in their section on the sacramentality of the anointing of the sick. The statement of Trent reads as follows:

> The sacred anointing of the sick was instituted by Christ our
> Lord as a true and proper sacrament of the New Testament.
> It is alluded to indeed by Mark, but is recommended to the
> faithful and promulgated by James the apostle and brother

of the Lord.[46]

In 1551, the bishops at the Council of Trent had only a small under-standing of the history of the Christian sacraments. Moreover, they in-terpreted the gospels in a very a-historical way. In the gospel of Mark, the bishops found a text indicating that Jesus alluded to the sacrament of anointing, but it was in the letter of James, an apostle and a broth-er of Jesus, that the bishops found the institution of the sacrament of anointing the sick. James is referred to as a "priest" πρεσβυτερος.

Thomas Leahy, in his commentary on *The Epistle of James*, notes that πρεσβυτερος is understood as follows: "Elders were likewise ap-pointed over the missionary churches. Thus the term does not signify merely advanced age, but an official position of authority in the lo-cal church."[47] Leahy, along with most other biblical scholars, does not state that the πρεσβυτερος was an "ordained priest." Rather, he was a leader in a Jesus community around the year 70 C.E. From this time to the Age of Charlemagne, lay people anointed the sick as well as deacons and priests.

A major change in the sacrament of the anointing of the sick took place during the Carolingian Reform which was begun by Charlemagne (742-814) himself. This reform movement lasted until 1100 C.E. Char-lemagne had inherited a part of Europe—the Frankish lands—which had a patchwork of laws and traditions. Little by little, the leaders of his reform unified the laws and traditions of these colonies. One of the foci of these reforms was the sacrament of the anointing of the sick. In this reform, the anointing of the sick was connected to sin, and since only a priest could forgive sin, lay people, in this reformation, could no longer anoint the sick in a sacramental way. Andrew Ciferni states the changes in a solid way:

The gradual clericalization of the rite had much to do with

the evolution of the sacrament of Penance, or Reconciliation. Because of the rigorous demands made upon those who entered into public penance during the first eight centuries and the fact that it could be received only once in a lifetime, Christians tended to postpone entrance into this state until close to death. Because the sacrament of anointing was reserved to those who were in full communion with the Church, it necessarily needed to be delayed until after deathbed Reconciliation. Thus the development of the continuous rite of Penance, Anointing of the Sick, and Viaticum (the final reception of Holy Communion) – were all administered by a priest.[48] From the beginning of the ninth century, down to the Second Vatican Council, the anointing of the sick was actually the anointing of those who were near death. The renewal of the sacrament of anointing made by Vatican II was one of the more successful changes in the liturgy. For eleven hundred years, anointing of the sick was almost exclusively an anointing of a Christian at the point of death, and since this sacrament of anointing also forgave sins, only a priest could anoint a dying Christian. Vatican II changed the rite to an anointing of the sick, but it did not change the position that only priests could anoint the sick.

In the early centuries, Christians brought a small amount of oil in a cruet of some sort to the church when they came for Mass. These cruets of oil were blessed by the priest or bishop, and the people took their blessed oil home with them. They anointed members of their families who were sick and even anointed themselves when they were not sick. Lay ministry for those who were ill had become a major part of the Church's mission. In the citation above, we see that historically the anointing of the sick became a sacrament of forgiveness of sin and therefore it was reserved to priestly ministry. Vatican II widened its use so that all sick Christians could be anointed, but the bishops maintained that the anointing had to be done by a priest.

These changes in the area of who can receive the sacrament of anointing, who anoints, and when can anointing take place are historical facts. If one claims that Jesus instituted this sacrament, how can there be radical changes in the administration of this sacrament? For centuries, this sacrament was administered in a way that Jesus did not intend. In an overview of this sacrament that we find in Section Two of the *Catechism,* there is no adequate mention of the changing issues that has affected the history of this sacrament.

6. The Sacrament of Holy Orders, a Sacrament at the Service of Communion

The title of this section of the *Catechism* is "The Sacrament of Holy Orders." This is followed by a theological explanation of the term orders, which begins with Jesus who is the priest par excellence.[49] All baptized share in the priesthood of Jesus. In an essentially different way, the ordained ministers share in the priesthood of Jesus and at the same time they are at the service of the common priesthood. For those who are ordained, the terms ministry and service frequently appear in the text. The sacrament, therefore, is called "Two participations in the one priesthood of Christ" (§1553).

The historical development of episcopal ordination, priestly ordination, and diaconal ordination is lengthy and complicated. An entire section in the *Catechism* offers a historical development of bishop (*episkopos*) and priest (*presbyteros*), namely, §§1539-1571. However, the *Catechism's* history of *episkopos* and *presbyteros* is not based on a thorough reading of the New Testament or on the writings of earliest Christian authors.[50] Rather, the authors maintain a historical view of priesthood and episcopacy which contemporary historical theologians and other scholars have carefully revised.

The bishops at Vatican II did not want to enter into the history of *episkopos, presbyteros,* and *diakonos* as these ministries developed in the early Christian Churches. A changing of this history was not the main focus of the conciliar bishops, so they simply avoided the complications of this history.

One might think, however, that a *Catechism* written thirty years after Vatican II might include a fairly thorough presentation of ordained history. The conciliar bishops can be excused, since their main focus was the development of a revised theology of church. Authors of a *Catechism*, however, appear not quite reliable when they focus on ordained ministry and do not offer an adequate historical base for the changes in ordained ministry from the end of the second century to the end of the twentieth century. At the end of the second century and the beginning of the third century, we have the first document on ordination of bishop, priest, and deacon. In my own book on the priesthood, I make the following summary:

> From the time of the resurrection to the beginning of the third century, we have hardly anything at all on the issues of ordination. The issue is, however, quite complex, even though there is practically no documentation at all during the first two centuries. Part of the problem lies with the development of the episkopos in East and West. Dupuy mentions that in the West a collegial presbyterium for both the episkopos and presbyter was dominant, while in the East a monarchical form of episkopos dominated.[51]

In the *Apostolic Tradition* of Hippolytus (cc. 170-236) we have the first extant ordination ritual for an *episkopos*, *presbyteros*, and *diakonos*. This document was written in Rome, roughly around 215. Probably, the prayers for ordination could be dated a few decades earlier, and the author, Hippolytus, used them in his manuscript. When Hippolytus died, these ordination prayers did not enjoy much publicity. Perhaps, the ritual continued in Rome, but only after a hundred years do scholars find citations of these ordination rituals in other areas of church life.

Given the lack of historical verification for much of the data in the

Catechism's explanation of the early roles of *episkopos, presbyteros,* and *diakonos,* I will simply say that hopefully a more verified study of the early years of the sacrament of ordination will appear in the next revision of the *Catechism.* What is presented in this section of the *Catechism* cannot be seen as an adequate foundation for the sacrament of Holy Orders.

7. The Sacrament of Matrimony, a Sacrament of Service and Communion

The title of the final section is "Marriage in God's Plan." This sacrament has also been called "nuptial covenant," "marriage in the Lord," "the sacrament of the covenant of Christ and the Church," and "a sacrament of the New Covenant" (§§1601 – 1666).

The history of the sacrament of marriage has been carefully studied by many authors such as Joseph Blenkinsopp, Eric Fuchs, Theodore Mackin, John Noonan, Edward Schillebeeckx, and Kenneth Stevenson. In the works of all of these writers, the role of the Catholic Church and its relationship to marriage is carefully stated. The Gregorian reform of the church came to a close at the end of the eleventh century. The theology of marriage had been a part of the Carolingian reform, but it was only in the twelfth century that one can claim that marriage was accepted as a Christian sacrament. Some authors conclude that in the second Lateran Council, (1139), the Catholic Church first accepted marriage as a sacrament. However, it was actually in the Second Council of Lyon (1274) under Gregory X that marriage was officially named as the seventh and last sacrament of the church.

Once again, the material in article seven of the *Catechism* which deals with the sacrament of marriage does not take into consideration the history of the sacrament of marriage and the ways in which this history of marriage affects the understanding of marriage as a sacrament. Article seven of Section Two is constructed in the following way:

1. Marriage in God's Plan.
2. The Celebration of Marriage.
3. Matrimonial Consent.
4. The Effects of the Sacrament of Marriage.
5. The Goods and Requirements of Conjugal Love.
6. The Domestic Church.

The authors of this material on marriage as a sacrament do not take into account that marriage was not considered a sacrament until the thirteenth century. This late date raises serious questions regarding the institution of the sacrament of marriage by Jesus. It also raises serious questions regarding Christians who got married from the first century down to the thirteenth century. These issues are simply ignored.

There is a strong "theology of marriage" in the paragraphs of this section of the *Catechism*, and these strong points are very helpful to the Catholic women and men who today are considering marriage or who are living in a sacramental marriage. However, since marriage has not always been considered as a sacrament, one might ask: how unchangeable are the issues which are treated by the authors of this part of the *Catechism*? Sacramental history is not something we can simply set to one side. Rather, we must face up to the problems which the histories of each sacrament entail. Hopefully, in a revised edition of the *Catechism*, the historical questions for all the sacraments will be addressed in a more comprehensive and honest way.

VI. Conclusions

There are several conclusions which the material in this chapter allows us to make:

1. **A strong movement by leaders in all Christian communities**

took place from early 1900 onward to rethink the theology of Church, and this ecclesiological rethinking included a rethinking of sacramental theology in its interconnection to the theology of Church.

We see this in key Catholic theologians such as Schillebeeckx, Semmelroth, Rahner and Segundo. The majority of bishops at Vatican II were well aware of this urgent need to reconsider both ecclesiology and sacramental theology. One of the leading issues for the reformation of ecclesiology at Vatican II was the development of a more intense union of ecclesiology to Christology and to Trinitarian theology. The documents of Vatican II move strongly in this direction. Today, every presentation of the sacraments needs to include the interrelationship of the church as a sacrament with a theology of the seven sacraments.

2. **In 1966, one year after the closure of the Second Vatican Council, William Baraúna, a peritus of the Council, edited a two volume publication, entitled *The Liturgy of the Vatican II*.[52] The essays in this volume clearly indicate that the bishops at Vatican II stated that the church itself is a sacrament.**

The symposium of contributors included some the best liturgical scholars at that time, most of whom had been theologians who had attended the council. In the essays of this book, the authors comment on every liturgical issue which was changed by the conciliar bishops. Giacomo Cardinal Lercaro wrote the Foreword, and in his writings he commented on the conference presentations. He states: "While this study, which has been lovingly made by many minds, is opportune at the present time, it will be such even more tomorrow when the seed sown by the Constitution [on the liturgy] will have blossomed."[53] Lercaro challenges us today to study what the council fathers changed vis-à-vis liturgy and sacramental celebrations and to see whether the bishops' changes have been taken seriously fifty years later. Lecaro is asking immediately after the Vatican Council to do what this present volume is meant to be, namely, a contemporary reconsideration of whether the sacramental life in the church, as presented at the Second Vatican Council, has been accomplished during the past fifty years. Is the leadership of the Catholic Church, both official leadership and theological leadership, fulfilling in 2014 what the conciliar bishops presented in the documents of Vatican II?

For the most part I think that the leaders have done much to change the pre-Vatican II theological understanding of sacrament to the newly expressed theological understanding of sacramental life. However, it is also true to say that major conservative elements in the church, both official and theological, have not allowed the seeds established by the conciliar bishops to blossom. Cardinal Lercaro would consider this negative situation a rejection of the Second Vatican Council.

3. **The *Catechism of the Catholic Church* offers two different approaches to sacramental theology: the first theology of the sacraments is based on the Trinity and on *Christus totus*; the second theology of the sacraments is based on the traditional pre-Vatican II teaching on the sacraments.**

There are two different approaches to sacramental theology in the *Catechism of the Catholic Church*. The fact that there are two approaches to sacramental theology indicates that in the post-Vatican II period there has been both a strong conservative movement and a strong progressive movement in the Catholic Church. The *Catechism* has become doctrinally formative in many dioceses, since some local bishops require the use of the *Catechism* for the RCIA, confirmation preparation, and diaconal preparation. Other local bishops do not require the *Catechism* as the textbook for religious education. This two-fold stance indicates an on-going struggle in the Catholic Church for a return to a pre-Vatican II Church on the one hand and on the other hand openness to the documents of Vatican II.

The two approaches to sacramental life which one finds in the *Catechism* cannot avoid confusion. One might say that a return to the pre-Vatican II theology of the sacrament is allowed because of the *Catechism*, but one might also say that the two different approaches to sacramental life which one finds in the *Catechism* need to be totally reconsidered.

4. **Not only has sacramental theology been changed during the past fifty years, the sacramental liturgies of the Catholic Church have also been reformulated in the fifty years after Vatican II.**

In spite of the liturgical norms established in the constitution on the sacred liturgy, *Sacrosanctum Concilium* (§§21-46), the Vatican Curia has, during the past fifty years, restricted cultural adaptations of sacramental liturgies, the translations of liturgical books, and the pastoral adaptations of sacramental liturgy which the global Catholic Church needs. However, since there are differing views on sacramental theology, there are also differing views on the liturgical celebration of the sacraments. In some parishes, the liturgical celebrations follow a conservative format which stresses the seven sacraments, while in other parishes the liturgical celebrations follow a format that expresses the church as a basic sacrament. It is not a question of obeying church authority; rather, it is a question of different theologies of sacramental life in the church.

5. **The scholarly history of the seven sacraments, which has been thoroughly investigated since 1896, challenges the view that Jesus, in his lifetime, instituted all seven sacraments.**

The historical research on each is touched upon here and there in this chapter, but by and large the historical findings on each of the sacraments is disregarded or mentioned in a brief way and usually in small print. For the meaning of the small print, see *Catechism*: §20.

The history of the sacraments, as we shall see in chapter four, has raised numerous questions about Jesus' institution of all seven sacraments. For five of the sacraments, we have no early data at all. Only from the second century to the fourth century do we have the first texts, which are not always clear, describing the celebration of the sacraments of reconciliation, orders, confirmation, and anointing of the sick. For baptism, see §1240 in which the Eastern Liturgies have not and do not use the phrase "I baptize you." They do use the phrase: "The servant of God, N. is baptized in the name of the Father, of the Son, and of the Holy Spirit." This is a wonderful example of the sacramental liturgy – work of the Holy Trinity.

In the presentation of each individual sacrament, another series of questions appears in Section Two explaining each of the sacraments. The question reads: "How is the sacrament celebrated?" The answers are found in the following paragraphs.

Baptism: §§1229 ff.

Confirmation: §§1297 ff.

Eucharist: §§1345 ff.

Reconciliation: §§1434 ff.

Anointing of the Sick:1517 ff.

Holy Orders: §§1539 ff.

Marriage: §§1621 ff.

For each of the sacraments, there is a description of the manner in which the sacramental action is celebrated today. Once again, in none of these pages do we read that the "liturgy is the Work of the Holy

Trinity." Nor do we read that God the Father blesses and blesses and blesses us in each of the liturgical celebrations. We do not read that Jesus is central in each of the liturgical celebration nor do we read how overwhelming the work of the Holy Spirit is. The material from Section One (§§1077-1109) is not presented as the heart of the above sections on "How is the sacrament celebrated?"

My conclusion regarding Section Two on the sacraments in the *Catechism* is that the sacramental material as presented in this section is basically a repeat of pre-Vatican II sacramental theology. The authors do bring in material from the New Testament and from the Vatican II documents, but when one considers the theological positions in each of the divisions of Section Two, one finds a repetition of the standard pre-Vatican II sacramental theology.

Let us move to chapter two, which centers on three major theological traditions in the Western Roman Catholic Church. In the second section of part two of the *Catechism*, which was analyzed above, the theological tradition behind the material is basically Neo-Thomistic, which is simply one form of Thomism. Religious educators frequently teach classes in sacramental theology in and through one of the three western theological traditions: the Augustinian tradition, the Thomistic tradition or the Franciscan tradition. They may not be aware of the specific theological tradition; however, a given tradition dominates much of the sacramental material presented in religious education classes. For instance, if the second section of the *Catechism* is used as the basic text for a class, the Neo-Thomistic tradition unites the material whether the teacher or the students realize this fact or not. Consequently, in chapter two we will consider the three theological traditions which have deeply affected the theology of the sacraments during the fifty years after Vatican II.

Endnotes

1. Edward Schillebeeckx, *Christus: Sacrament van de Godsonmoeting* (Bilthoven: H. Nelissen, 1960).

2. Edward Schillebeeckx, *Christ the Sacrament of the Encounter with God*, Eng. trans. by Cornelius Ernst, (New York: Sheed and Ward, 1963).

3. On the issue of "Jesus of History," see John Meier, "Jesus," in *The New Jerome Biblical Commentary* (Englewood Cliffs, NJ: Prentice Hall, 1990), 1316-1328. Meyer correctly indicates that the issue of the "historical Jesus" is a contemporary issue: "The 'Jesus of History' is a modern theoretical reconstruction – a fragmentary, tentative portrait painted by modern scholars – and is not to be identified naively with the full reality of the Jesus who actually lived in the 1st cent. AD (the 'real Jesus')," 1317.

4. Schillebeeckx, *Christ the Sacrament of the Encounter with God*, 13.

5. Ibid. 15.

6. See Karl Rahner, *Kirche und Sakramente* (Freiburg im B, Germany: Herder, 1963); Eng. trans. by W. J. O'Hara, *The Church and the Sacraments* (New York: Herder and Herder, 1963). Rahner presents the saving presence of the humanity of Jesus as a sacrament. In the English translation, Rahner writes: "God is reconciled to the world. There the grace of God appears in our world of time and space. There is the spatio-temporal sign that effects what it points to. Christ in his historical existence is both reality and sign, *sacramentum* and *res sacramenti*, of the redemptive grace of God" 15. However the main focus of Rahner's book is on the sacramental structure of the church. The above citation on the humanity of Jesus as a sacrament is the only reference to this theme in his volume.

7. In the second half of Schillebeeckx's book, he discusses the basic issues of sacramentality: matter and form, minister and recipient, etc. He explains these issues in a way similar to the sacramental presentation in the *Summa* of Thomas Aquinas. There seems to be two distinct parts to his book, and the two parts are not well integrated.

8. Otto Semmelroth, *Vom Sinn der Sakramente* (Frankfurt a. M: Verlag Josef Knecht, Carolusdruckerei GmbH., 1960). Eng. trans. by Emily Schossberger, *Church and Sacrament* (Notre Dame, IN: Fides Publishers, 1965).

9. Semmelroth, *Church and Sacrament*, 13.

10. Ibid. 16.

11. Ibid. 28.

12. Ibid. 35.

13. Ibid. 39.

14. Ibid. 13-19.

15. Ibid. 19-28.

16. Ibid. 28-34.

17. Ibid. 9-10.

18. See Karl Rahner, *The Church and the Sacraments*. Notice especially his opening statements which define his position on the church as a sacrament, 11-32. My references will be to the English translation of this book.

19. Karl Rahner, "Zur Theologie des Symbols," *Schriften zur Theologie*, band IV (Einsiedeln: Benziger Verlag, 1962), 275-311, especially 299-300.

20. Ibid. 7.

21. Ibid. 9.

22. Juan Luis Segundo, *The Sacraments Today* (Maryknoll, NY: Orbis Books, 1974). See "Introduction," 3. In my own volume, *Sacramental Theology: A General Introduction* (New York: Paulist Press, 1988), 12, I mention that Segundo's volume is more focused on the church than on the sacramental rituals However, I also state that the works by Segundo and Boff are of tremendous value for sacramental theology. "Christological presuppositions shape ecclesiologial presuppositions which again shape the sacramental theology. With major works in Christology, the liberation theologians are establishing the basis for a more detailed sacramental theology down the line." See Osborne, *Sacramental Theology: A General Introduction* (New York: Paulist Press), 16-17.

23. Segundo, op. cit., 3.

24. For the Latin text, I am using *Sacrosanctum Oecumenicum Concilium Vaticanum II: constitutiiones, decreta, declarationes* (Vatican City: Typis Polyglottis Vaticanis, 1966). For the English text, I am using *The Basic Sixteen Documents Vatican Council II: constitutions, decrees, declarations* (Northport, NY: Costello Publishing Company, 1996), General Editor: Austin Flannery.

25. See the *Latin-English and English-Latin Dictionary* by John T. White (Chicago: Follett Publishing Company, 1928), 634.

26. See John H. Miller, ed., *Vatican II: An Interfaith Appraisal* (Notre Dame, IN: University of Notre Dame Press, 1966).

27. Charles Moeller, "History of *Lumen Gentium's* Structure and Ideas," in *Vatican II: An Interfaith Appraisal*, 124-126.

28. Gerard Philips, "The Church: Mystery and Sacrament," in *Vatican II: An Interfaith Appraisal*, 187-196.

29. See Carlo Colombo, "The Hierarchical Structure of the Church," in

Vatican II: An Interfaith Appraisal, 209. His entire article, 208-218, is focused on the sacramental constitution of the church, and on the basis of ecclesial sacramentality he explains the hierarchical structure of the church.

30. Session IV, "Discussion," in *Vatican II: An Interfaith Appraisal*, 176-184; the comment on primordial sacrament can be found on 177.

31. *Catechism of the Catholic Church*, second edition (Vatican City: Libreria Editrice Vaticana, 1997). In the following pages, this book will be referred to as *CCC*.

32. *CCC*, n. 1076, p. 280.

33. The relationship between a theology of the Trinitarian God and sacramental issues will be explained in detail in chapter four of this volume.

34. In *CCC*, n. 1140, there is a long passage from the Vatican II document, *Sacrosanctum Concilium*, §§ 26 and 27. Moreover, in *CCC*, n. 1141, there are citations from *Lumen Gentium*, §§ 10 and 34 and also from *Sacrosanctum Concilium*, n. 14.

35. Bonaventure Kloppenburg, *A Ecclesiologia do Vaticano II*, Rio de Janeiro: Editora Vozes Limitada, 1971; *The Ecclesiology of Vatican II*. Eng. trans. by Matthew O'Connell (Chicago, IL: Franciscan Herald Press, 1974), 19.

36. Ibid. 21.

37. The paragraph expressing Kloppenburg's description of the sun and moon is based on Kenan Osborne and Ki Wook Min, *Science and Religion: Fifty Years after Vatican II* (Eugene, OR: Wipf & Stock, 2014), chapter six.

38. In the 1960s, there were many books and articles written on the question whether or not the early Christian community baptized infants. See for instance K. Aland, *Did the Early Church Baptize Infants?* Eng. trans. by G. R. Beasley Murray (Philadelphia: Westminster, 1963); Joachim Jeremias, *Infant Baptism in the First Four Centuries*, Eng. trans. by D. Caines (London: SCM Press, 1960); Joachim Jeremias, *The Origin of Infant Baptism*, Eng. trans. by Dorothea M. Barton (London: SCM Press, 1963). The questions regarding infant baptism in the first four centuries have never been totally resolved. However, it appears that in most parts of the Christian world, during the first six centuries, the non-baptism of infants was the more common practice.

39. For a detailed and lengthy discussion on the catechumenate, see Kenan Osborne, *The Christian Sacraments of Initiation*, (Mahwah, NJ: Paulist Press, 1987), chapter two, "Holy Baptism and the New Testament," 24-61 and "Holy Baptism and the Early Church," 62-78.

40. See CCC, n. 1266 in which the authors mention that the Trinity is present at baptism and gifting the one who is baptized. However, in

the cross-references for n. 1266, no reference to Section One, §§ 1077-1109 is made which is entitled "The Liturgy – Work of the Holy Trinity."

41. *CCC*, n. 902.

42. Paul VI was not in favor of these words, since they focused solely on the meaning of a term, and not on the reality.

43. In the *Catechism*, cross references are found in the margins, and they refer to another part of the *Catechism*. The authors of Section Two make the following references to paragraphs in Section One. These cross-references are basically focused on the use of the same word or the same phrase. They are not based on the theology of Section One, which involves *The Liturgy – Work of the Holy Trinity* and *Christus totus*.

n. 1236 refers to n. 1102, but the linking of these two sections is on a very general issue of faith and its proclamation.

n. 1253 refers to n. 1123, and the connection seems to be the repetition of the phrase "sacrament of faith."

n. 1257 refers to n. 1129. The connection is the use of the same phrase "necessary for salvation. In 1257, baptism is necessary for salvation, and in 1129 "the sacraments" are necessary for salvation.

n. 1296 refers to n. 1121; both paragraphs refer to an "indelible mark on the soul."

n. 1304 refers to n. 1121 and for the same reason the two sacraments produce a character on the soul, which is another expression for the "indelible mark on the soul."

n. 1326 refers to n. 1090, and in both paragraphs the phrase "heavenly liturgy" is found.

n. 1327 refers to n. 1124, in which both n. 1124 refers to belief and prayer and n. 1327 refers Eucharist. The connection is not clear.

n.1328 refers to n. 1124, in which God the Father is blessing us. However, in n. 1328 the authors do not refer to God the Father as blessing. It does refer to Jewish blessings.

n. 1330 refers to n. 1169. In 1330, the entire paragraph centers on the Eucharist; in 1169 the focus is on Easter. It is unclear where there is a mutual relationship.

n. 1333 refers to §§ 1147 and 1148. In all three paragraphs there is a mention of creator.

The above are simply examples of the referencing in the CCC. There are another 23 cross references, but by now the reader should have a clear understanding of these references, namely that they are mostly references to similar words or small phrases; they do not refer to the theology of Section One.

44. See Kenan Osborne, *Reconciliation and Justification: The Sacrament and its Theology*, (Mahwah, NJ: Paulist Press, 1990) for a detailed and lengthy presentation of the history of reconciliation.

45. See Hermas, *Commandment*, 4, 3, in which the author states that there is only one opportunity of post-baptismal reconciliation. Check also 4.1 and 4.8. Hermas does not indicate any ritual. His emphasis is on the personal prayer of the sinner for God's forgiveness, but if this was all there was, the allusion to the role of the church community makes no sense. His writing was used by a number of later church leaders, and they seemed to have understood Hermas as announcing some sort of liturgical format. Hermas was not a theologian, nor was he a man of great education. However, in his view the church of Jesus was a church that reflected the mercy of God.

46. The Council of Trent, session XIV, 1551: see Henry Denzinger, *Enchiridion Symbolorum, Definitionum et Declarationum de Rebuse Fide, et Morum*, (Freiburg in Br.: Herder, 1963), n. 1695.

47. See Thomas Leahy, "The Epistle of James," *The New Jerome Biblical Commentary*, 915.

48. See Andrew Ciferni, "Anointing of the Sick," *The HarperCollins Encyclopedia of Catholicism*, ed. Richard McBrien, (San Francisco: HarperSanFrancisco, 1995), 58.

49. At this juncture of the *CCC*, n. 1536, the authors refer the reader to the section on ministry in the Church in *CCC*, §§ 874-896. In this section, the focus is on priestly ordination. In *CCC*, §§ 1586 to 1600, the authors focus on priestly ministry.

50. Among many other writings, see Kenan Osborne, *Priesthood: A History of the Ordained Ministry in the Roman Catholic Church* (Mahwah, NJ: Paulist Press, 1988).

51. Osborne, op. cit., 119.

52. William Baraúna, ed., *The Liturgy of Vatican II*, Eng. ed., edited by Jovian Lang (Chicago: Franciscan Herald Press, 1966).

53. See Giacomo Cardinal Lercaro, "Foreword," *The Liturgy of Vatican II*, xii.

CHAPTER TWO

Sacramental Theology within the Three Western Theological Traditions

Jesus lived his entire life within a Jewish religious world; a world that was simultaneously under Roman rule with its Latin language and thought patterns, and influenced by both Greek language and Greek thought. Languages are more than a means of communication. Each language has its overtones and undertones of cultural philosophies and religious tendencies. Cultural individuality is developed in many ways through languages, and cultural identity is a subtle component of each and every language. In reading the New Testament, we are presented with the cultures in which Jesus lived, namely the Judaic culture of his time, the Roman/Latin cultural influence of his time, the Greek cultural influence of his time, and even the Arabic culture to some extent.

The development of the Jesus community after his death and res-urrection provides us with the same issues of cultural diversity. The New Testament writers wrote in Greek, therefore subtle Greek mean-ings of words and phrases are present in the New Testament writings. Most of the authors, however, were Jewish, and so we also notice Jew-ish ways of thinking even though they are expressed in the Greek lan-guage. Since the Palestine was under Roman rule at the time of Jesus and the New Testament writers, the early followers of Jesus were also under a Latin-language influence.

At the end of the first century C.E. and into the second century, many followers of Jesus lived in the Latin-speaking world. In time, some of these followers of Jesus began writing about Jesus and the Jesus communities in Latin. These writings were the beginning of what we today call the writings of the Western Fathers of the Church. The followers of Jesus who lived in Greek-speaking communities also began writing in Greek about the gospel message, and these early Greek writings were the beginning of what today we call the writings of the Eastern Fathers of the Church.

In the course of time, patristic literature – writings of the fathers – became literary traditions. There was and still is a Western Latin tradition of Christian literature. There is also an Eastern Greek tradition of Christian literature. However, in both the Latin and Greek traditions, differing forms of philosophical and theological interpretation began to appear, and with the multiplicity of languages in the Eastern Churches a number of traditions developed: namely a Syriac theological tradition, a Coptic theological tradition, an Armenian theological tradition, a Russian theological tradition, etc.

In the western world, three major theological traditions gradually took hold. The three traditions are the Augustinian tradition, which developed from the teaching and writings of St. Augustine of Hippo, the Thomistic tradition, which developed from the writings of Albert the Great and Thomas Aquinas, and the Franciscan tradition, which developed from the spirituality of Francis of Assisi and the writings of such scholars as Alexander of Hales, Bonaventure and John Duns Scotus.

There are different traditions in other areas of human endeavors such as literature, science, history, and art. Theology and philosophy are no different. A tradition focuses on forming an interconnection for all the facets of a given field, such as art, literature, philosophy and theology. In western theology, the Augustinian tradition provides a way of uniting the various aspects of Christian life. So, too, the Thomistic tradition weaves together the various aspects of Christian life in a different format. The Franciscan tradition does the same thing.

In these three traditions, the articles of faith are maintained but the interconnection of the articles of faith with one another is formulated in differing patterns. Consequently, all three traditions have been honored and respected in the history of the western Catholic Church even though all three traditions formulate three different summations of Catholic faith.

In the history of the western Catholic Church, almost all major theologians have presented their teachings in and through one of the three traditions. We can also say that Catholic educators over the centuries have also taught their students Catholic theology, and they, too, have expressed this theology in and through one of the three traditions. The Vatican has consistently honored these three differing traditions as acceptable ways in which the Catholic faith is presented. At the Council of Trent, for instance, there were bishops and theologians who urged an Augustinian approach to certain church teachings. At the same time, there were Thomistic and Franciscan bishops and theologians who urged the interpretations of their respective traditions. In the discussions at Vatican II, Augustinian, Thomistic, and Franciscan theological positions were all part of the bishops' discussions. At Vatican II, especially in the final texts of *Lumen Gentium* and *Gaudium et Spes*, the bishops carefully avoided any dominance of one tradition over the other. The bishops most often presented a biblical approach or a more generalized and open approach.

Today, Catholic religious teachers present the Catholic faith within of one of these philosophical/theological frameworks, whether they realize it or not. This includes Catholic teachers' explanations of the sacraments. The material in this chapter is simply a summary of the three traditions in and through which Catholic sacramental theology has been presented over the past centuries.

Chapter Two is divided in the following way:

I: The role of the three major theological traditions in the western church.

II: The Augustinian theological tradition.

III: The Thomistic theological tradition.

IV: The Franciscan theological tradition.

V: Conclusions

I. The Role of the Three Major Theological Traditions in the Western Roman Catholic Church

In the Western Roman Catholic Church, the three major theological traditions, the Augustinian tradition, the Thomistic tradition, and the Franciscan tradition, are still very present. Western Catholic theology has been in great measure established within the framework of all three of these traditions. Those who teach or preach or write about sacraments must realize that these theological traditions have shaped and will continue to shape the ways in which the sacramental presence in the church is presented.

During the fifty years after Vatican II, scholars have written abundantly on the writings of Augustine of Hippo. In 1962, Frederick B. Artz published his volume, *The Mind of the Middle Ages*, which appeared in print in the very same year that Vatican II began.[1] In 1964, Eugene Kevane, published his volume, *Augustine the Educator: A Study in the Fundamentals of Christian Formation*. The Schiller Institute Conference, which took place in Rome in 1985, testifies that Augustine remains meaningful down to today. In 1985, the proceedings of this conference were published in *Saint Augustine: Father of European and*

African Civilization.

During the fifty years after Vatican II, scholars have written abundantly on the Thomistic theological tradition. In his volume, *Thomas Aquinas: Theologian*, Thomas O'Meara, a major contemporary Dominican theologian, presents a seven-page bibliography that contains an abundance of material written in the past fifty years by scholars on the Thomistic tradition.[2]

During the fifty years after Vatican II, scholars have also written much about the Franciscan tradition. Prior to Vatican II, critical texts of the writings of Francis of Assisi, Clare of Assisi, Alexander of Hales, Bonaventure, Scotus, William of Ockham, and many other Franciscan scholars were developed. With these critical editions, a second wave of material appeared in print that focused on the Franciscan philosophy and theology of each author. Much of this philosophical and theological material was published within the last fifty years.[3]

The *Catechism of the Catholic Church* is an example of a presentation of doctrine within a Western theological tradition. In his apostolic letter, *Laetamur Magnopere*, John Paul II makes the following statement describing the purpose of the *Catechism*:

> The Catechism confirms its purpose of being presented as a full, complete exposition of Catholic doctrine, enabling everyone to know what the Church professes, celebrates, lives, and prays in daily life.[4]

Catholic scholars state that in the Catholic Church there is no one full, complete exposition of Catholic doctrine; rather, the various expositions have been shaped by each of the Augustinian, Thomistic and Franciscan theologies. The Augustinian tradition—as a theological and philosophical tradition—began to develop in a clear way from the eighth century onward. The Thomistic and Franciscan traditions began to develop in a clear way from the fourteenth century onward.

All three traditions have been profoundly influential in the Catholic Church and they are still profoundly influential in today's Catholic Church. The way in which the *Catechism* presents the Catholic faith is primarily a presentation within the Thomistic tradition and in a secondary way within an Augustinian tradition. The *Catechism* does not use the Franciscan tradition in any of its presentations.

It is helpful to note that in the Eastern Christian Churches, there are several other major theological traditions. The main Eastern Christian theological traditions include:

1. The Byzantine Orthodox tradition

2. The Armenian Orthodox tradition

3. The Coptic Orthodox tradition

4. The Nestorian Orthodox tradition

5. The Persian Orthodox tradition.

The central, foundational and unchangeable beliefs of the Christian life are maintained in all of the traditions, both Eastern and Western.[5] However, at the theological and philosophical levels through which the details of Christian beliefs are more fully explained, there are major differences among all of the above traditions.

In the Western world, there are also Anglican and Episcopalian traditions, Lutheran traditions, Presbyterian traditions, Evangelical Church traditions and Free Christian Church traditions. In these non-Catholic traditions, the Augustinian tradition is often strongly present. We see this in the *Thirty-Nine Articles of Religion* (1571) and in the *Book of Common Prayer* (1549). Scripture, of course, is the fundamental source of Anglican faith, but in the theological explanation of the scriptural faith, Augustinian theology is very evident. The same combination of scripture and Augustinian theology is found in the writings of Luther and Calvin. A theological tradition is unavoidable, since by itself, scripture needs some form of further explanation more often than not.

In all of the churches mentioned above, there are sacramental celebrations, particularly the celebrations of baptism and Eucharist. The explanation of these sacramental rituals by various church leaders in the non-Catholic churches have been generally developed based on scriptural passages and, to some extent, the Augustinian theological tradition.

The main focus of this chapter is the sacramental theology of the Western Catholic Church. To accomplish this, we should note that the Western Catholic Church has never had a single theological and philosophical theology of sacraments.[6] Each of the three main theological traditions has presented an acceptable theological and philosophical explanation of the sacraments. As a result, Catholic theology on the sacraments has never been uniform, and this non-uniformity of theological positions remains acceptable in today's Catholic Church.

Theological and philosophical traditions require a lengthy period of time to develop historically. In the remainder of this chapter, I will analyze the Augustinian tradition, the Thomistic tradition, and the Franciscan tradition. In doing so, the reader can see that each tradition has moved through four distinct stages of development. The first stage centers on the founder or founders of the tradition. The second stage occurs immediately following the death of the founder or founders during which the founder's writings are preserved. The third stage takes place when the theology and philosophy of the founder or founders begin to be accepted within the academic world. The fourth and final stage takes place when the theology and philosophy of the founder or founders are fully accepted within the academic world as a major philosophical or theological tradition.

In the three major theological traditions of the Catholic Church, there is also a gradation of doctrines in which certain higher doctrines shape the more secondary doctrines.

1. The Doctrine of a Trinitarian God

The first and most important doctrine within an individualized tradition is the way in which a tradition presents its theology of a Trinitarian God. Each particular tradition, the Augustinian, the Thomistic, and the Franciscan, has a different theology of the Trinitarian God, and this God-theology structures all other aspects within a given theological tradition.

2. The Doctrines of Creation and Incarnation

The second most important aspect of the three theological traditions is intrinsically complicated, since this aspect focuses on the relationship between a theology of creation and a theology of incarnation. In Catholic theology, an understanding of the incarnation makes no sense at all unless it is conjoined to a theology of creation. Likewise, in Catholic theology, an understanding of creation makes no sense at all unless it is conjoined to a theology of the incarnation.

The three theological traditions have formed their own theologies of creation-incarnation, and each of these positions is theologically acceptable within the wider Catholic community. Since the three theologies of creation have been expressed on the basis of their distinct theologies of a Trinitarian God, the distinct theologies of the Trinitarian God have shaped the ways in which the Augustinians, the Thomists, and the Franciscans have developed their theologies of creation and incarnation. In each tradition, the theologies of Trinity, creation, and incarnation are intimately bonded with each other.[7]

3. The Doctrine of Salvation

Each particular theological tradition offers a theology of salvation. The Augustinian theology of salvation, the Thomistic theology of salvation, and the Franciscan theology of salvation are different, and this difference arises from basing their respective theologies of salvation on their respective theologies of God, of creation and of Jesus.

4. The Doctrines of Human Life, Church, Sacraments and the "Last Things"

Only on the basis of the above three fundamental issues has each particular theological tradition offered a theology of human life, a theology of church, a theology of the sacraments, a theology of the "last things." All of these particular theological issues are shaped by their respective theologies of God, their theologies of creation and incarnation, and their theologies of salvation.

There is a hierarchy in the theological issues that each theological tradition develops, but in this hierarchy of theological issues each tradition regards its theology of God, its theology of creation and Jesus as well as its theology of salvation as the foundational aspects of its respective position. Consequently, the theology of sacraments in Augustinianism, Thomism and Franciscanism is influenced and structured by deeper and more intensive theological issues than the sacraments themselves. The sacramental differences on a theology of sacraments are based on their respective theological differences regarding the Trinitarian God, creation-incarnation, and salvation.

To present a clear theology of sacraments in a classroom, therefore, an instructor needs to take into account the theological tradition in and through which he or she is presenting his or her class on sacramental theology. The instructor needs to realize that in his or her teaching of the sacraments there is also, at least indirectly, a teaching on a particular theology of the Trinitarian God, a particular theology of creation, a particular form of Christology, and a particular theology of salvation and church. Because of this interrelationship, it is important for teachers in the Western Christian Church to see how each of the three major traditions has been intrinsically operative over many centuries of church life.

It takes a lengthy period of time for a theological and philosophical tradition to develop. In the period of development, there are clear stages through which an intellectual tradition slowly comes to fruition.

Stage One: The Beginning of an Intellectual Tradition

The life and times of the person provide the names or nationalities the tradition bears. As regards a theological tradition in the Western Church, there have been three major theologians who have been the originators of the three traditions: namely, Augustine (354-430), Thomas Aquinas (1225-1274), and Francis of Assisi (1181-1226). Even though other personages were involved in the development of the three traditions, the names of each of these men have been selected as the main originator of the three traditions: the Augustinian tradition, the Thomistic tradition, and the Franciscan tradition. At this initial stage, one cannot as yet speak of a tradition, since the focus is simply on a single individual who in his life time was either a major teacher or a major founder.

Stage Two: The Initial Steps of an Intellectual Tradition

Following the death of a founder, an intellectual tradition begins to be developed embryonically by an immediate group of followers who have retained his writings, have acquainted others with his views, and have begun to develop his philosophy or theology in a more systematic way. At this stage of development, however, one cannot speak as yet of a theological tradition. One can only say that there is a small beginning of a "school" of thought, based on the theology and philosophy of the founder.

Stage Three: The Slow but Sure Growth of the Founder's Positions

It is the efforts of a later group of theological and philosophical scholars that establish the founder's positions within the academic world. In other words, the theological and philosophical teachings of the founder slowly become more acceptable within the academic framework. However, at this introduction of material into the wider academic world, we still do not have a "theological tradition." The academic world might not encourage the founder's positions, and consequently no intellectual tradition will arise. His or her writings will remain historically interesting but they will have little to no continuing influence. However, if there is a solid interest in the founder's positions, a rootage in the academic world will begin to take place.

Stage Four: The Academic Acceptance of an Intellectual Tradition

Gradually, if members of the academic world who are presenting the philosophical and theological positions of the founder gain widespread and lasting credibility within the academic world, an intellectual tradition has reached its birth. From then on, the presence of the particular tradition will develop within the academic framework and will sometimes branch into an even greater maturity and diversity of tradition.

Many contemporary books on the sacraments, my own included, begin with specific sacramental issues, such as "The Sacrament of Baptism," or "The Sacrament of Eucharist." In the opening chapter of these books, a theology of God or a theology of Trinity is already presupposed. In the opening paragraphs, there are no indications regarding the ways in which one's theology of God/Trinity shapes and formulates the individual sacraments.[8]

In 1970, Anne Hunt wrote a book on God as part of the series of "Theology in Global Perspective." Her book is entitled *Trinity: Nexus of the Mysteries of Christian Faith*.[9] This title is profoundly intriguing since the title indicates that the Trinity is the centering or nexus for the mysteries in our faith, including the sacramental mysteries. She describes this interconnection as follows:

> The novelty of this book resides in its exploration of the methodology of interconnection, which has been comparatively neglected in relation to the methodology of analogy in the history of theology. Our precise aim in this book is thus to explore and present the Trinitarian nexus or interconnection of the mystery of the Trinity with the other great mysteries of Christian faith.[10]

Her major issue has been well expressed, for today one cannot simply state that there is a basic nexus between the Trinitarian God and the God who is central to baptism, confirmation, Eucharist, etc. A simplistic comment on interconnection is no longer viable, since such simplicity leaves Catholic life in a fragmented way. There is a major interrelationship between one's belief in God and one's belief in sacramental life. Hunt is deliberately showing that the theology of Trinity is the basic nexus which draws together any and every theological tradition, and this includes any and every sacramental theology.

All three of the major intellectual traditions in the Western Catholic Church have historically passed through these four stages of development. A brief overview of their stage by stage formation can be of help to today's teachers in sacramental theology. We will first consider the beginning, growth, and development of the Augustinian theological and philosophical tradition. We will then consider the beginning, growth, and development of the Thomistic theological and philosophical tradition and will finally consider the same for the Franciscan theological and philosophical tradition.

II. The Augustinian Theological Tradition

The developmental stages of the Augustinian tradition can be seen in the following outline. The Augustinian tradition has a basic structure, but there are many sub-forms of this one tradition, such as the Augustinian traditions found in the writings of Peter Lombard, Anselm of Canterbury, Richard of St. Victor, etc. Therefore, when one speaks of an Augustinian tradition, the title includes the many sub-forms of the Augustinian tradition.[11]

There are four stages that took place in the development of the Augustinian tradition:

1. The Life of Augustine (354-430)

In the life of Augustine, there was a development of his own personal understanding of Christian theology. His early education in Carthage and his subsequent teaching in Italy can be considered as a beginning of his intellectual life. This includes his philosophical readings of Neo-Platonists. His conversion and baptism to Christian faith took place in 387. In 391, he was ordained to priesthood, and he was consecrated as bishop of Hippo in 395. From this period on, Augustine slowly became a major theological teacher of the early church. His theological writings increased enormously and he engaged in a series of theological conflicts. In his conflicts with the Donatists and with the Pelagians, he experienced conflict over predestination, original sin, and the power of the bishop of Rome. He took time to not only be a teacher of theology but also the author of many theological writings. He died in 430. Keep in mind that during his life, an Augustinian tradition had not yet formed.

2. The Immediate Followers of Saint Augustine

Augustine's first followers were those who kept copies of his writings. Orosius was a leader in this process after Augustine's death. His own work, *Seven Books of History Against the Pagans*, carried out Augustine's focus on education. Orosius' work became the standard text on history for the schools throughout Europe. Gradually, some of these followers began to use Augustine's writings in their own catechetical and educational work. This required a frequent re-copying of his writings as the number of such teachers and students multiplied. At this period in time, one can begin to see the initial appearance of a possible theological tradition. Augustine's writings were often copied by monks, thereby more and more people became aware of Augustine's theology. In these years, the groundwork of a theological tradition had begun.

3. The Theological Tradition of Augustine Begins to Show Signs of a Permanent Tradition

Stage three began to take place in the ninth century, when Benedictine monks became organized and popular teachers. From 927 to 1157, many Benedictine abbeys had established theological schools. Cathedral schools also developed during the eleventh century. In these schools, theological professors used the writings of Augustine as their major texts. These initial school systems, which were founded throughout Europe, provided the solid basis for the Augustinian theological tradition. Slowly but surely, Augustine's writings became standard within the European academic world. In many ways, Augustine had become "the theologian of the Church" for western Catholicism. Tertullian and Cyprian were still read, but it was Augustine's writings that had become the foundation of academic theology in the

West. During this time, however, the bible was the main text used for theological classes. Augustine's theology was only used in a way that explained biblical texts. It was in the late twelfth century and the early thirteenth century that a theological text, *the Sentences of Peter Lombard*, became the textbook used in the universities of Europe.

4. The Augustinian Theological and Philosophical Tradition Becomes an Intrinsic Part of Western Church Thinking

In the twelfth century, the academic world of cathedral schools and monastic schools throughout Western Europe included professors who taught theology and philosophy based on the writings of Augustine, which lead to his theology and philosophy becoming common throughout the educational centers of Europe. The Augustinian theological tradition clearly influenced all major theologians in the thirteenth and fourteenth century, including Peter Lombard[12] and it strongly influenced the Catholic bishops and theologians at the Council of Trent.

The Augustinian theological tradition influenced the post-Trent development of seminaries for priestly academic and spiritual formation, which began in 1641 with Jean-Jacques Olier and his religious community to St. Sulpice. Seminary professors were slowly required to use theological text books that had been approved by the Vatican. These theological text books contained an extensive amount of Augustinian theology.

The Augustinian theological tradition is still influential in today's Roman Catholic Church, which is evident in the *Catechism of the Catholic Church*, which cites Augustine more than any other theologian, namely, there are 87 citations from St. Augustine. St. Thomas Aquinas is the next with 60 citations while St. Bonaventure has only 3 citations.

•••

Augustinian theological and philosophical thought has been operating as a major Christian Tradition in the Western Christian Churches for the past twelve hundred years.[13] Its long-lasting presence in the churches is a major indication of its value and integrity. Given the major changes in human intellectual life which have taken place in the last one hundred years, the Augustinian theological tradition will perhaps carry less weight, but there is no indication that it will disappear.

In the history of Trinitarian theology, Augustine's theology of Trinity has influenced almost all major Western theologians down to the twentieth century. We find evidence of this Trinitarian influence in the *Catechism of the Catholic Church*. Today, Augustine's theology of the Trinity remains active within the Catholic and Protestant framework. However, his Trinitarian theology has been changed and adapted both theologically and philosophically as we shall see in the Trinitarian theology of Thomas Aquinas.

Augustine's arguments with the Manichaeans, the Donatists, and the Pelagians are not always clear. At times, there is a deep pessimism in the writings of Augustine, which tend towards a negative attitude regarding human nature itself. According to Augustine, only in and through baptism is a person removed from a state of sin. The removal from sin raised the delicate question: who is saved and who is not saved? Augustine has been accused of a form of predestinationism. His responses to this accusation have not totally vindicated his position. Not only was predestination a difficult matter in the fifth century, it also affected the Calvinists in the sixteenth and seventeenth centuries. At the Synod of Dort (1618-1619), a strict form of predestination was upheld, and Arminius, who maintained a softer view of God's predestination, lost out. His views were later accepted by the Methodist and Baptist Churches. Because of these theological altercations,

Augustine's views on salvation, on Jesus' death, on creation and even on the nature of God have engendered different approaches to Christian life. These differences have affected the theology of sacraments at times gently but at other times more fiercely.

III. The Thomistic Theological Tradition

The Thomistic theological and philosophical tradition passed through the four stages mentioned above regarding the Augustinian theological tradition. In stage one, the founders of the Thomistic tradition, namely Albert the Great and Thomas Aquinas, who were both university professors, wrote many lectures and treatises, which they used in their classwork and which contained the primary theology and philosophy of both scholars. In stage two, after the death of Albert and Thomas, Dominican friars who had studied under them gathered together the writings of these two scholars, after which the ideas of Albert and Thomas were kept alive primarily within the Dominican Order. At the third stage, other Dominican professors at the European universities began to base their own lectures on the works of Albert and Thomas. Through these professors, the Thomistic tradition gradually became part of the curriculum in some universities. Finally, a large number of universities, primarily Dominican schools, had established a chair of Thomistic studies which resulted in the Thomistic tradition becoming widespread.

The Dominican theologian Thomas O'Meara has provided us with a lengthy and detailed history of this development in his book entitled *Thomas Aquinas: Theologian*.[14] In chapter one, O'Meara presents an overview of Thomas Aquinas' early life and his life with the new order of Dominicans. Thomas was born between 1224-26 and he died in 1274. His intellectual mentor, Albert the Great, played a major role in

Thomas's academic formation. Thomas studied at the universities of Paris and Cologne, and subsequently taught in Paris, Naples, Orvieto, Rome, and Viterbo. Thomas Aquinas was clearly a major intellectual person during his lifetime, and his writings bear witness to the depth of his philosophical and theological acumen. When he died, there was as yet no Thomistic intellectual tradition, but stage one of the eventual formation of the intellectual tradition which bears his name offers us a man of tremendous intellectual acumen.[15]

The influence of Augustine is clearly evident throughout the writings of Albert the Great and Thomas Aquinas but the two scholars developed a new form of the Augustinian tradition, which we call the Thomistic intellectual tradition. The Thomistic tradition is new because of the far-reaching presence of the philosophy of Aristotle in the works of Albert and Thomas.

In a way similar to the tradition of Augustine, the Thomistic tradition has had a number of sub-forms. O'Meara traces the main "Thomisims" in his chapter, "Traditions, Schools, and Students," which presents in great detail the many sub-schools of the Thomistic philosophical and theological tradition.[16]

Over the past six hundred years, three major aspects of the Thomistic tradition have had a highly positive and enriching effect on the theological and philosophical world of the Catholic Church. The three aspects of this new form are: 1. the strong Aristotelian framework of the tradition; 2. the comprehensiveness of Thomas' *Summa theologiae*; and 3. the unifying strength of the Catholic tradition from the Reformation down to the time of Euro-American secularization.

Thomas' theologies of the Trinitarian God, Christology, creation, and salvation have clearly affected the theology of sacraments in the Western Church. In recent times, there have been Thomists who were extremely closed vis-à-vis contemporary European culture and there have been Thomists who were very open to contemporary culture. In his volume, *Thomas Aquinas, Theologian*, Thomas O'Meara presents in some detail the "Thomist Spectrum."[17] These differing interpretations of Thomas' theology affected the theology of sacraments which was taught in the twentieth century by the open-minded Thomists and which was taught in that same century by some closed-minded Thomists. Moreover, since Thomism dominated Catholic Theology from the time just after the Council of Trent down to the middle of the twentieth century, and since Catholic Thomistic theology during that period of time was rigidly apologetic and dismissive of Christian Churches which did not accept the papacy, there was a rigid interpretation of the sacraments. This rigidity is clearly present in the four-volume work, *Sacrae Theologiae Summa*, published basically by the Jesuits from the University of Salamanca, Spain.[18]

In my view, however, the Thomistic tradition has been very helpful to Catholic thinking in the following ways.

1. The Thomistic tradition has carefully structured its theological material within an Aristotelian philosophical base.

A first major contribution of Thomas was his consistent and over-arching use of Aristotle's philosophy. In a very deliberate way, Albert the Great and Thomas Aquinas brought the philosophy of Aristotle into Catholic theology.[19] Up to the twelfth century, Latin translations of the writings of Aristotle were limited. Boethius (480-524) had translated into Latin only Aristotle's *Categoriae* and *De Interpretatione*. However, in the twelfth century a number of scholars, primarily in Spain, began translating Aristotle into Latin either from the original Greek or from Arabic translations. By 1250, almost all of Aristotle's works had been translated into Latin.

The abundant use of Aristotle's philosophy is a key innovative part of the Thomistic tradition. The presence of Aristotle in the writings of Albert the Great and Thomas Aquinas is a major element in the differentiation of the Augustinian and Thomistic traditions. Augustine, who did not know the Greek language, has never been considered a theologian influenced by Aristotle. Rather, his philosophy was derived in great measure from Plotinus and through Plotinus he learned something of the philosophy of Plato. Thus, the acceptance of Aristotle's philosophy by both Albert and Thomas gives the Thomistic intellectual tradition a remarkable and distinctive position in the academic world.

It is important to note that both Albert and Thomas in some way or another "baptized" Aristotle. For instance, Aristotle did not consider the "Prime Mover" as a divine reality, while Albert and Thomas did envision the "Prime Mover" as God. For Albert and Thomas, it was necessary to baptize the entire system of Aristotle in and through their emphasis on first cause, who is the God of creation.[20] The brilliance of Aristotelian philosophy remains strong throughout the writings of Albert and Thomas. The brilliant use of Aristotle's philosophy is clearly a major characteristic of the Thomistic intellectual tradition.[21]

2. The Thomistic tradition has presented the church with a "Summa of Created Life," namely a life which has come from a loving and creator God.

A second major contribution of Thomas was his production of an outstanding *Summa theologiae*. Thomas wrote his *Summa theologiae* at the end of his life, and in this *Summa* he presents a strongly unified understanding of the earthly world and the heavenly world. His all-embracing world-heaven view is clearly a major characteristic of the

Thomistic intellectual tradition. Thomas used the philosophy of Aristotle, which is also world-oriented, to help us understand a world created by a Trinitarian God.

In many ways, entering into the Aristotelian world view is similar to entering a cul-de-sac, because Aristotle touches on almost all areas of created reality. When one enters into the Thomistic *Summa*, there is also a sense of a cul-de-sac, since one is surrounded by all created reality and by the Creator of all created reality. Thomas' *Summa* is meant to show us what our universe and, to some degree, what God's own existence are all about. *Summa* is an excellent word to describe Thomas' goal. The brilliance of the *Summa* is clearly a second major characteristic of the Thomistic intellectual tradition.

3. The Thomistic tradition has provided the Catholic Church with a unity of philosophical insights and theological beliefs within a coherent program, and from Reformation times on, this unified doctrine has provided the Catholic Church with a strongly unified intellectual framework, which became a strong bulwark in its stance toward Anglican, Protestant, and Free Church theologies.

A third major contribution of Thomas Aquinas was the presence of his philosophy and theology in the Roman Catholic Church from the Reformation to the middle of the twentieth century. This contribution, however, needs major explanation. The Thomistic theological and philosophical tradition had been highly honored from the fourteenth century to the sixteenth century. In all of Christian theology up to the sixteenth century, there was no specific treatise on the church. Naturally, theologians used the term church frequently, but no one had developed a "treatise of the church."

With the Reformation, various churches claimed to be The Church. Theologians such as Robert Bellarmine defended the Roman Catholic

Church as the only true church. Ecclesiology, in its specific format, became a theme for Anglican scholars, Protestant scholars, Free Church scholars and Catholic scholars that lasted from the aftermath of the Reformation down to the beginning of the twentieth century. All denominations wrote ecclesiologies in which the authors "proved" that their church was the true church of Jesus Christ. Catholic ecclesiologies were based on the theology of Augustine and even more so on the theology of Thomas, and this gave a unified theology of church as Catholic leaders and scholars continued to teach that only the Roman Catholic Church was the one true church. Thomism, taken in a wide scale, provided the Catholic Church with a unified ecclesiology.[22]

From the beginning of the twentieth century onward, there has been a different approach to ecclesiology. We have seen above that contemporary ecclesiology in the theologians and in the conciliar bishops was founded on a Trinitarian base and on a Christological base. The ecclesiology found in the documents of Vatican II is a major Catholic step away from a defensive position toward an open position.

In the sixteenth century, a major event occurred in the Western Christian Church that splintered the Christian world, namely, the Reformation. The Council of Trent took place from December 13, 1545 to December 4, 1563. Three years later, in 1566, the *Catechism of the Council of Trent* was published, and this *Catechism* was strongly Thomistic. Charles Borromeo also published a *Catechism* that became very popular throughout the European Catholic Church. His *Catechism* relied on the theology and philosophy of Thomas Aquinas in a very comprehensive way. In local and general congregations of the Jesuits which took place in the late 1500s, the leaders of the Jesuit community prescribed that the theology and philosophy of Thomas Aquinas was to be used in all Jesuit schools throughout the world. Jesuit educational institutions gradually appeared in all sections of the world, and the resulting Catholic teaching, which was expressed in Thomistic terms, affected all parts of the seventeenth and eighteenth century Catholic Church.

From the Council of Trent onward, Western Christianity—Anglican, Catholic, and Protestant—became very apologetic. There was extreme pressure on the Catholic Church to maintain its integrity in spite of the areas throughout Europe in which Protestantism had taken over. In the late 1700s and throughout the 1800s, a secularization of Europe and the United States gradually gained power. The Vatican and episcopal leaders of the Catholic Church continually tried to present a united front, a goal for which the dominance of Thomistic theology was of great assistance. All theological textbooks which would be used in seminaries had to be approved by the Vatican Curia and these theological textbooks basically adhered to Thomistic theology. The bishops in several national conferences authorized local *Catechisms* which were to be used in the schools under their jurisdiction. The *Baltimore Catechism* became the central source of Catholic religious teaching throughout the United States. These catechisms were also Thomistic.

From 1900 onward, however, other factors began to enter the intellectual life of the Roman Catholic Church and the Thomistic unity slowly began to wane. These new issues were diverse; some the main issues are the following:

1. The rise of ecumenism from its early beginnings in Scotland to the formation of the World Council of Churches. Respect for religious differences began to lessen the usual religious perception that "only our church is the true church." This also moved into a wider ecumenism which began to lessen the usual religious perception that "only our religion is the true religion."

2. The emergence of new scientific findings such as quantum me-

chanics and the age of the universe. These two issues, along with the theory of evolution, revolutionized contemporary science and created a chasm between science and history.

3. The history of the sacraments of the church which began in 1896 with the publication of H. C. Lea's volume, *A History of Auricular Confession and Indulgences in the Latin Church.*[23] This anti-Catholic book stimulated Catholic scholars to investigate the history of all seven sacraments of the Catholic Church. This historical research on the sacraments was thorough and revealing. Even today, in the twenty-first century, there are scholars who are researching the history of the Christian sacraments.

4. The appearance of post-modern philosophies, some of which stressed the inter-relational structures of all reality, as well as the inconsistencies between religious positions on salvation history and the newly-discovered cosmic universe of the twentieth century.

5. The rise of an appreciation of cultural differences, which included a respect for cultural philosophies and morality. Christian Churches, whether Anglican, Catholic or Protestant, and whether Western or Orthodox, were seen as culturally hidebound. An openness to other cultures and other religions is still increasing today at a very fast pace.

Other issues could be added to this list, but the above issues have challenged the Roman Catholic Church in a serious way. The Thomistic tradition as well as the Augustinian tradition and the Franciscan tradition have gradually lost ground. Vatican II was heralded in many ways as a council that would open the Catholic Church to the world in which we live, move and have our being.[24]

IV. The Franciscan Theological Tradition

A similar format of stages to that of the Augustinian and Thomistic traditions can be found in the development of the Franciscan theological and philosophical tradition. This tradition developed at the same time in which the Thomistic tradition developed, namely in the thirteenth and fourteenth centuries. In some ways the two traditions are in tandem with each other, but in other ways, the two traditions move in totally different directions. Let us consider the points of difference first and then take up the points of similarity.

1. The Title of the Tradition, namely, the "Franciscan Tradition"

Francis of Assisi was in no way an academic theologian. The Augustinian tradition bears the name, Augustine, who was a highly gifted theologian and teacher. The Thomistic tradition bears the name, Thomas, who was also a highly gifted theologian and teacher. Why is the Franciscan tradition not named after one of its own highly gifted theologians and teachers such as Alexander of Hales, Bonaventure, or John Duns Scotus?

Within the Franciscan tradition, as we shall see, there are theological distinctions such as Bonaventurianism and Scotism, but both of these are sub-titles for respective parts of the Franciscan theological and philosophical tradition. Moreover, spirituality is not synonymous with either theology or philosophy. The questioning as regards the naming of this tradition provides us with the first major difference between the Franciscan tradition on the one hand and the Augustinian and Thomistic traditions on the other hand. The title, Franciscan tradition, provides us with the first major distinctive facet of the Franciscan theological and philosophical tradition, namely: Franciscan spirituality imbues the entire framework of Franciscan philosophy and theology. In the Franciscan approach, one cannot separate Franciscan spirituality from Franciscan philosophy and theology.

In the Augustinian tradition, Augustine's spirituality does not accompany the theology and philosophy of Augustine as it moves through the historical stages described above. Rather, the spirituality of the Benedictine monks began to maintain the writings of Augustine, and the spirituality of the monks was Benedictine and not "Augustinian." When Albert the Great and Thomas Aquinas, both Dominican friars, began to construct the beginnings of the Thomistic tradition, there is no mention of Dominic or Dominican spirituality. The same cannot be said for the Franciscan enterprise. Spirituality accompanied the development of a Franciscan theological and philosophical tradition from the start. The Franciscan theological and philosophical tradition is unique in many ways because of the integrating presence of Franciscan spirituality to Franciscan philosophy and theology.[25]

2. The Franciscan Theology of a Trinitarian God

Théodore de Régnon (1831-1893), in his volume, *Études de théologie positive sur la Sainte Trinité*, claimed that there were only two scholastic approaches to the Trinity.[26] On one hand, there was Bonaventure's interpretation rooted in Dionysius, Richard of St. Victor, William of Auvergne, William of Auxerre and Alexander of Hales, and on the other hand there was Thomas' interpretation based on Augustine, Anselm of Canterbury, Peter Lombard and Albert the Great. Zachary Hayes summarizes the difference between these two Trinitarian theologies in the following way:

> [As regards] the fundamental difference between the two he (de Régnon) traces to the dynamism of the neo-Platonic thought in the first line and the static character of Aristotelian thought in the second.[27]

Olegario Gonzalez, in his volume, *Misterio Trinitario y existencia humana: estudio histórico teológico en torno a San Buenaventura*, was one of the early scholars who brought about a change from De Régnon's position.[28] Through his analysis of both Richard of St. Victor and Bonaventure, Gonzalez indicates that Bonaventure's Trinitarian doctrine is not based on the Trinitarian theology of Richard of St. Victor. Rather, Bonaventure' Trinitarian doctrine is strongly based on the Dionysian tradition of the Greek Church, which Bonaventure had learned from his own teacher, Alexander of Hales. Consequently, Bonaventure's approach represents a major third Christian view of Trinity in the Western world. The Western Christian Church has a Trinitarian theology from Augustine, a second Trinitarian theology from Thomas, and a third Trinitarian theology from Bonaventure.

Bonaventure consistently offered a theological view of a relational God, but he also continued to use non-relational words in respect to God. These non-relational words were commonly used in the scholastic period, namely: one, only one, one nature, one essence, one substance, immutable, and *summe simplex*. However, Bonaventure also used an abundance of relational terms when he described the Trinitarian God, namely: ability to produce, eternal production, emanation, communicability, powerful, fontal fullness, infinitely free love, positive relationship, primal fountain, etc. Bonaventure's theology of the Trinity centers on God who is characterized by the following phrase: *"bonitas est sui diffusiva"* (goodness is diffusive of itself). Divine love, which is a continually diffusing love, is the basis of Bonaventure's theology of the Trinitarian God.[29]

Bonaventure's theology of the Trinitarian God is basic to the Franciscan intellectual tradition. All other aspects of the Franciscan tradition are shaped and formed by Bonaventure's theology of the Trinitarian God. This influence of a relational Trinitarian God in the Franciscan tradition is carefully detailed in the volume by Johannes Freyer, *Homo Viator: Der Mensch im Lichte der Heilsgeschichte.* Freyer offers a subtitle which describes his volume: *"Eine theologische Anthropologie aus franziskanischer Perspective."*[30]

The Franciscan theological tradition is centered on a relational, loving, and self-giving understanding of a Trinitarian God. This theology of God gives the Franciscan theological tradition an originating and distinctive form. The Franciscan tradition, based on the spirituality of Francis and Clare, is primarily rooted in its theological center, the Trinitarian God of relational love.

3. The Franciscan Emphasis on the Infinity of God as expressed in the Theology of John Duns Scotus

Bonaventure died in 1274 when John Duns Scotus (1265-1308) was only eight years old. In many ways, Scotus, at the end of the thirteenth century, became a major theologian in the early development of the Franciscan theological and philosophical tradition, for he enriched the tradition with new elements and new insights. Scotus' philosophy and theology affected three key areas of the Franciscan tradition: (a) the Franciscan theology of the Trinitarian God, (b) the Franciscan theology of creation, (c) and the Franciscan theology of incarnation.

a) The Franciscan theology of the infinite Trinitarian God

Bonaventure taught that everyone, if they were true to themselves, believed in God. If some people denied God, their denial was based on their own lack of moral integrity. The position of John Duns Scotus was different. Scotus asked himself whether or not it was possible to prove that something actually infinite exists. Allan Wolter states the case very clearly:

> Is the Existence of God Self-Evident? This question is partic-
> ularly pertinent in view of the objective Scotus sets for him-
> self, viz. to prove that something actually infinite exists. For
> the very notion of being actually infinite implies existence.[31]

According to Wolter, Scotus realizes that other theological positions on the existence of God had been expressed and even accepted.
However, these theological positions are not all that strong. Wolter explains the situation as follows.

> In the present life no notion we possess of God such as "nec-
> essary existence," "infinite being," or the famous Anselmian
> description "a being greater than which nothing can be con-
> ceived," will satisfy the requirement of the subject of a self-
> evident position.[32]

Wolter is paraphrasing and clarifying a passage from the *Ordinatio*
which was written by Scotus. The citation from Scotus reads:

> If you ask whether to be is predicable existentially of any
> (proper) concept which we conceive of God, so that the prop-
> osition in which existence is asserted of such a concept is self-
> evident ... I say no.[33]

For Scotus, such notions are all constructs and there is no basis for
us humans to say that something or someone is infinite. The proposi-
tion that "An infinite being exists" cannot be demonstrated *a priori* by
a demonstrative argument. At this juncture, Scotus differs from Thomas Aquinas and Henry of Ghent. For these two scholars, "being" exists
first, and only in a secondary way can a person apply descriptive adjectives to "being" such as "all-knowing," "almighty," and "infinite."
Scotus argues that the very essence of God is infinite, and therefore
God is not first a supreme being and secondly other adjectives, such as
infinite. For Scotus the very being of God is infinite. If God is infinite,
there can only be one God, since two infinities are contradictory.

When Scotus was working on his philosophical and theological
essays and lectures, Christianity was the dominant and dominating

religion in Europe. The followers of Judaism were present in the European cities, but they were few in number compared to the Christians. The Islamic people were also known and active, but they existed on the fringes of Europe and the Europeans judged their number in a minimalistic way.

Today, this is not the case. In 2007, Christians were about one-third of the world population. This percentage of Christians has diminished in the past six years. In 2013 there are about 7.4 billion people on this earth and it is estimated that by 2083, there will be 10 billion people on this earth. The majority of this growth in the human population will not be Christian, since the growth will be most evident in the Asian countries, in the sub-Saharan African countries, and in the Islamic countries.

These mathematical figures raise a question about the theology of God. If the one God creates so many people who are not Christian, how can Christians say that there is only one God, namely the Christian God? How can religious Jews claim that Yahweh is the one and only God? How can religious Muslims claim that Allah is the one and only God? How can so many people whom God has created be left to one side? This extensive rise in world population today cannot help but challenge the theology of God in all three Abrahamitic religions.[34]

If God is infinite, no single religion today can limit God to his or her religion. Today, we are in a very different world-view than Augustine, Thomas, and Scotus. We are in a different world-view than Abraham, Moses, David and Solomon. We are in a different world-view than Mohammad and the Muslim leaders of the recent past. If God is infinite, then no human has any possibility of understanding the fullness of God.

This does not mean that the major world religions and the minor world religions have no validity. The center of each religion is not the religion itself, the church itself or the denomination itself. All of these communities offer a "glimpse" of the beauty of God to some grouping of people. Since the beauty of God is infinite, a person can only see a glimpse of God's beauty in and through his or her religious denomination. Today, we need to rethink what an "infinite God" means since God in his love has created all people. Christians, Muslims and Jews—even combined—will not constitute even half of the world population in 2083. The infinite God will still love all others, just as he loves members of the three religions of Abraham. This is a new complication for an understanding of an "infinite God."

b) Franciscan theology unites creation and Christology

Johannes Freyer, in his volume, *Homo Viator: Der Mensch im Lichte der Heilsgeschichte*, carefully and in detail explains Scotus' understanding of creation and the ways in which creation is fundamentally related to the incarnation.[35] First of all, Scotus strongly bases his approach to God on two scriptural texts: Exodus, 3:14: "I am who am" and 1 John, 4:16: "God is love, and whoever remains in love remains in God and God in him."

The first citation, "I am who am," is seen by Scotus as the first principle and the ultimate goal of all being. God is the absolute oneness in God's own self. God is life itself and the source of all created life. God is, therefore, always a creator even if no creation exists. God does not become a creator when God first creates, for God himself is creative power.

The second citation, "God is love," indicates that actual creation takes place because of God's love. God loves the world and God loves us into being. God's love is the womb of creation, and God's love is totally free.

On the basis of these two citations, Scotus turns to Christ as the image of the Trinity. Freyer calls this: "In Christus Abbild der Trinität." This relationship of the incarnation to God's primacy and God's love indicates that creation and incarnation are intimately united in the theological vision of Scotus. The incarnation did not occur as a saving event because Adam and Eve had sinned. Rather, the incarnation was conjoined to God's original loving plan to create. Scotus does not see Adam and Eve as the high-point of creation. Rather, Scotus finds the incarnation of the God-Man, Jesus, the high point of creation, that is, the very reason why there has been any creation at all.[36]

God's love is totally free, and even in the situation of human sin, God's love and forgiveness are totally free. Augustine taught that the personal sin of Adam and Eve and the original sin brought about by Adam and Eve needed to include a paying back to God, a redemption. It was Jesus who came as an incarnate redeemer, but Jesus and incarnation became necessary after the sins of Adam and Eve. Scotus totally rejects this view. God's love is the womb of creation and also the womb of the incarnation, and God's love is totally free. Sin did not cause the incarnation.

c) The Franciscan Emphasis is on Relationality rather than on Essence or Substance

The plurality of persons in God belongs to the infinity of God. The infinite God is infinitely relational. Like Bonaventure, who has a single page on the existence of God and six hundred pages on a relational God, Scotus begins with an infinitely relational God who is one, since there cannot be two infinite Gods.

Augustine needed to establish divine immateriality in order to make a clear division between uncreated nature and created nature. Only on the basis of divine immateriality was Augustine able to speak about common operations and the spiritual aspirations of those touched by God. Thomas Aquinas needed to place "the plurality in the relations outside the divine essence and calling the persons subsisting relations." Divine essence is explained in the *Summa Theologica* where Thomas establishes the divine essence from Quaestio II to Quaestio XXVI, which involves 136 pages in Peter Caramello's edition of the *Summa Theologica*. Only in Quaestio XXVII from page 137 onward does Thomas turn his attention to the trinity of persons.

Both Bonaventure and Scotus move in a totally different direction. When they begin to speak of God, they begin to speak of an infinite God and a relational God. God is relationally three in an infinite way and God exists in an infinite way as well. God's nature is infinitely relational in the approach of both Bonaventure and Scotus.

●●●

The three western theological/philosophical traditions have dominated Catholic theology from the time just after Augustine down to Vatican II. The three traditions have three different approaches to the Trinitarian God. In the next chapter, we will consider the section from the *Catechism* which includes the elaboration of the liturgy – work of the Holy Trinity. Our focus in chapter four will be on the way in which a Trinitarian tradition provides a foundation for the Trinitarian basis of all liturgies including sacramental liturgy.

V. Conclusions

The material of this chapter was presented more as a reminder than as a statement of something new. As a reminder, I wanted simply to restate that every theological position is generally elaborated through the prism of a theological tradition. This is not meant to be a negative statement; rather it means that western theology has been deeply enriched by three major theological traditions and that these theological traditions help us see how a given theology of sacraments can and should be united to a theology of God, a theology of creation, a theology of incarnation, etc. The traditions help us to unify our theological endeavors.

On the basis of this positive value of all three traditions, we can draw together several important conclusions.

1. The Western Catholic World has been blessed with three major theological traditions. Each tradition, however, has several subdivisions, which means there are differing forms, namely the Augustinian form, the Thomistic form, and the Franciscan form.

In the documents of Vatican II and in the *Catechism of the Catholic Church* there are different levels of Christian doctrine placed before us. In a generalized way, the doctrines of the Catholic Church fall into three categories.

Category One: Teachings of Faith that must be accepted by all Catholics

Catholic theologians often refer to a book called "Denzinger." This book is a compilation of teachings by the Catholic Church and it was initially organized by Henry Denzinger in 1854.[37] In the index of this volume, the reader finds an explanation of the importance or classes of various teachings. If the teaching is classified through a number written in bold type, then the particular statement is a solemn teaching of the Catholic Church. These solemn teachings must be accepted if one wants to remain within the Catholic Church.

Category Two: Official teachings which require obedience but which can be changed

A second rating is given to teachings of the Church which are obligatory at a given time, but which can be changed. An example of this level of importance is a teaching found in the Code of Canon Law. Every law can be changed, but at a given moment of time the Catholic Church is following one law or another. Liturgical rituals, approved by the Vatican, are also examples of a set of teachings which must be followed but which can be changed. After Vatican II, liturgical laws were changed so as to meet the principles found in the documents of Vatican II.

Category three: Theological opinions by an approved theologian
The third and widest form of Catholic belief is centered on theological issues. These theological issues express a teaching in a way that theologically and philosophically makes sense. Most of the *Catechism of the Catholic Church* is an expression of theological positions, which in the Western world are generally part of the Augustinian tradition, the Thomistic tradition, or the Franciscan tradition. None of this material is binding; all of this material is simply an expression of a theological position.

The editors of the *Catechism* did not indicate in a clear way which teachings are defined doctrines and must be accepted, which teachings are Church positions at this moment of time and should be honored until there is an official change, and which teachings are basically theological positions. In the *Catechism*, most of the theological positions are either Augustinian or Thomistic. Very few, if any, are expressions of the Franciscan theological tradition.

For a Catholic instructor who is teaching a course on the sacraments, the *Catechism* has certain strong points, but it also has major weaknesses. The text of the *Catechism* does not distinguish between a teaching that has been defined and a teaching that is based on the Augustinian or Thomistic tradition. The Catholic teacher needs to sift through the material on the sacraments as found in the *Catechism* and clarify for the students which teachings are the solemn teachings of the Catholic Church, which teachings are valid now and must be followed but which can be changed or modified by future official declarations of church leadership, and finally which teachings are a matter of theological argument.

Since the *Catechism* will be used frequently in catechetical work, in preparation for the reception of a sacrament, and for training Catholic teachers, the three forms of intellectual acceptance are a matter of necessity, not just something that only those who are intellectually trained might understand. The *Catechism*, as it stands right now, is not a helpful guide to distinguish defined teachings, teachings which are currently binding, and theological interpretations.

2. From the Council of Trent in the sixteenth century onward, the various teachings of the Church have reflected the Augustinian or the Thomistic theological tradition.

In this chapter on the three western theological traditions, we can see that there are differing views on many theological issues. To confront the various Protestant teachings, the official church confined the authors of theological textbooks to maintain a common ground of belief. The official church has done this by allowing or disallowing certain theological textbooks to be used or not used. From the beginning of the nineteenth century down to the middle of the twentieth century, all theological textbooks for use in the seminaries needed the "imprimatur" of the Vatican. This control of textbooks meant that the same theological format would be established in every seminary and the teaching would be the same for diocesan seminarians, Jesuit seminarians, Franciscan seminarians, Dominican seminarians, etc. Since the official church had endorsed Thomas Aquinas, the Thomistic theological tradition became the one and only approach to seminary education.

In contemporary seminaries, there has been a change in this control of theology. Today, the theology courses in the seminary system are not all the same. Various professors have been teaching a theology course in which the documents of Vatican II play a major role. However, many issues in the documents of Vatican II can be further developed within an Augustinian tradition, a Thomistic tradition, and a Franciscan tradition. Since the three main theological traditions offer differing perspectives, it would be helpful if Catholic teachers themselves could appreciate the different traditions, since the majority of theological teachings are not "officially" defined teachings, nor are they "official teachings" as of right now. Most of the teachings stem from a theological tradition and are therefore not unchangeable. Positions expressed in the *Catechism* need to be more clearly assessed as solemn teachings of the church, official teachings as of now, or theological positions.

3. Many of the leaders of the Catholic Church after Vatican II have opened the church to multi-culturalism. *Sacrosanctum Concilium* set up norms for cultural changes in §§37-40, 54, 65, and 119.

This openness does not stop with learning a foreign language or learning the history of another culture. Rather, it means that we need to honor the ways in and through which other cultures think both theologically and philosophically. In many places, the local vernacular language is used, liturgical music reflects the musical cadence of a given culture, and cultural art forms are visible. However, there is something deeper going on in the forms of acculturation within the Catholic Church. Theologians and some church leaders are beginning to think through the gospel message via the cultural philosophy and theology of a given place. For example, efforts have begun in Asia to rethink the Catholic faith from the standpoint of Confucius, or Mencius, or Wang Yangming. The statements made by the Federation of Asian Bishops' Conference have little by little used Asian philosophical and theological themes to bring about an ecclesiology. Similar efforts have been made in the last four decades regarding African philosophies and theologies. Here and there, similar efforts have been made to enculturate native populations throughout the western hemisphere. Major questions arise. Can Catholic faith be expressed through a Hindu format? Can it be expressed through an Arabic-Islamic philosophy? If we cannot do so, then we need to face the issue that the Christian teaching is basically Euro-American.

The three theological traditions examined in this chapter are all "western" in both their philosophy and their theology. Post-modern philosophy, namely the philosophical thinking of Husserl, Heidegger, Merleau-Ponty, Ricoeur, Lacan, Derrida, and many others are all western forms of philosophy. Can we, as Catholic Christians, think not of but in a theology and philosophy which are fundamentally Asian, African, or Native Cultural? Can we go beyond the trappings of a given culture (music, art, language, etc.)? If we can do this, then the three western theological and philosophical traditions, Augustinian, Thomistic, and Franciscan, will be set to one side and a totally fresh approach to philosophy and theology will become center-stage for large parts of human life. As yet, these efforts are not yet center-stage, but with a growth in world population in the next fifty or sixty years, more human beings will be in the Asian, African, and Arabic world than in the Euro-American world.

Endnotes

1. See Eugene Kevane, *Augustine the Educator: A Study in the Fundamentals of Christian Formation* (Westminster, MD: The Newman Press, 1964), chapter eight, 257-288. See, also Whitney J. Oates, *Basic Writings of Saint Augustine* (New York, NY: Random House, 1948), especially the "Introduction," ix-xi, in which one finds a brief description of Augustine's philosophy and theology. The Schiller Institute Conference, which took place in Rome, 1985, testifies that Augustine remains meaningful down to today; see *Saint Augustine: Father of European and African Civilization* (New York, NY: New Benjamin Franklin House, 1985). See also, Frederick B. Artz, *The Mind of the Middle Ages* (New York, NY: Alfred A. Knopf, 1962), esp. 183-200.

2. See Thomas O'Meara, *Thomas Aquinas: Theologian,* (Notre Dame, IN: 1997), 290-296.

3. For the Franciscan tradition, see *The History of Franciscan Theology*, ed. Kenan Osborne (St. Bonaventure, NY: The Franciscan Institute Publications, 2007); see also Alfonso Pompeii, *San Bonaventura Maestro di Vita Francescana e di Sapienza Cristiana*, two volumes with essays by many scholars, (Rome: Pontificia Facultá Theologica San Bonaventura, 1976): see also *S. Bonaventura, 1274 – 1974*, five volumes with essays by many scholars (Grottaferrata, Rome: Collegio S. Bonaventura, 1972); see also *De Doctrina Ioannis Duns Scoti*, five volumes with essays by many scholars (Naples: Poligrafica & Cartevalori, 1968).

4. See John Paul II, "Laetamur Magnopere," CCC, second edition, xiv. In his Apostolic Constitution, "Fidei Depositum," John Paul had said the same thing, namely, that the CCC "is a statement of the Church's faith and of catholic doctrine, attested to or illumined by Sacred Scripture, the Apostolic Tradition, and the Church's Magisterium" (n. 3).

5. One of the most divisive issues between the Eastern Churches and the Western Churches and also between several Western Christian Churches is the issue of the papacy. This is a very complex issue and not all the dividing positions are based on matters of faith. Political and social circumstances have played a major causative role in these divisions. In recent times, church historians have studied the origins of the papacy in the early centuries of church life. For the complications involved in a theology of papacy, see Jean-Marie Roger Tillard, *The Bishop of Rome* (Westminster, MD: Newman Press, 1983); Patrick Granfield, *The Limits of the Papacy: Authority and Autonomy in the Church* (New York, NY: Crossroad, 1987); and Paolo Brezzi, *The Papacy: Its Origins and Historical Evolution* (Westminster, MD: Newman Press, 1958).

6. An important distinction in Catholic theology centers on the hierarchy of Catholic truths. There are three major classifications of these

truths. Some Catholic truths include articles of faith and official solemn teachings of the Church. These truths must be accepted as unchangeable. Some official teachings of the church include undefined but official teachings of the church leadership. These truths are official during a certain period of Catholic Church history but they can be revised. A third category includes acceptable theological positions. These latter have theological value but no normative value. Teachers are free to accept such theological positions as they see fit. For a detailed consideration of these three classifications of Catholic doctrine, see Kenan Osborne, *Sacramental Guidelines: A Companion to the New Catechism for Religious Educators* (New York, NY: Paulist Press, 1995), 1-17. On pp. 18-19, I have also presented a short statement which lists the major presuppositions which teachers and students bring with them into a class on sacramental theology.

7. Peter Lombard in his *Libri IV Sententiarum*, (Grottaferrata-Rome: Collegium S. Bonaventurae ad Claras Aquas, 1971), begins his study on the Trinitarian God, or God as God is in se. However, in Liber I, Dist. 14 to Dist. 18, he mentions the missions and the manifestations of both Logos and the Spirit. It may seem strange that in the middles of his discourse on God in God's own self, he brings up the missions and manifestations of the Logos and the Spirit. In many ways, Peter Lombard is indicating that the incarnation and the sending of the Spirit can only be understood in relationship to the nature of God. For Peter Lombard, his theology of the Trinity is reflected throughout all the other passages of his four-volume work. Since theological professors in the 13th and 14th centuries had to comment on Lombard's *Sententiae*, we have an abundance of explanations from that era on the way in which medieval theologians utilized a theology of Trinity to express all other aspects of Christian theology.

8. In the CCC, there are two ways in which the sacraments are presented. The first way presents the Trinity as the center of sacramental theology: Section One, §§ 1076-1209. The second way presents sacramental theology in the framework of Neo-Scholasticism, Section Two, 1210-1666.

9. Anne Hunt, *Trinity: Nexus of the Mysteries of Christian Faith* (Maryknoll, NY: Orbis Books, 1970).

10. Ibid. 3.

11. References to Augustine are innumerable. The following volumes are simply a selection of material which helps readers understand the theology and philosophy of Augustine. Étienne Gilson, *Introduction à l'étude de saint Augustin* (Paris: 1949); H. I. Marrou, *St. Augustine et la fin de la culture antique* (Paris: Éditions E. de Bocccard, 1958); Gustave Bardy, *A l'école de saint Augustin* (Ecully: Oeuvre Populaire d'Education, 1947); M. J. D'Arcy, ed., *A Monument to Saint Augustine* (London: Sheed and Ward, 1950); Gerhard Strauss, *Schriftgebrauch,*

Schriftauslesung und Schriftbeweis bei Augustin (Tübingen: J. C. B. Mohr, 1959); Nora Hamerman, ed., *Saint Augustine: Father of European and African Civilization* [Schiller Institute Conference, Rome, Nov. 1-3, 1985], (New York, NY: New Benjamin Franklin House, 1985).

12. See Paul P. Gilbert, *Introducción a la Teología Medieval* (Estella, Navarra: Editorial Verbo Divino, 1993), 49-69.

13. See Eugene Kevane, *Augustine the Educator: A Study in the Fundamentals of Christian Formation* (Westminster, MD: The Newman Press, 1964), chapter eight, 257-288. See, also Whitney J. Oates, *Basic Writings of Saint Augustine* (New York, NY: Random House, 1948), especially the "Introduction," ix-xi, in which one finds a brief description of Augustine's philosophy and theology. The Schiller Institute Conference, which took place in Rome, 1985, testifies that Augustine remains meaningful down to today; see *Saint Augustine: Father of European and African Civilization* (New York, NY: New Benjamin Franklin House, 1985). See also, Frederick B. Artz, *The Mind of the Middle Ages* (New York, NY: Alfred A. Knopf, 1962), esp. 183-200.

14. See Thomas O'Meara, *Thomas Aquinas: Theologian*, 1-40.

15. For an understanding of Thomas Aquinas, the introduction by O'Meara in *Thomas Aquinas: Theologian* is very penetrating and helpful, xi-xxi. In chapter one of this volume, O'Meara provides us with a detailed view of "Stage One: The Life of Thomas Aquinas," 1-40. Chapter Two, "Patterns in the *Summa theologiae*," 41-86, and Chapter Three, "A Theological World," 87-151, offer an in depth study of Thomas' philosophy and theology. In Chapter Four, "Traditions, Schools, and Students," O'Meara leads us through Stage Two: The Immediate Followers of Thomas, and Stage Three: The Beginnings of an Intellectual Tradition, 152-200. In chapter five, "Thomas Aquinas Today," O'Meara presents the powerful presence of the Thomistic Intellectual Tradition in the Western Catholic Church today, 201-243.

16. See O'Meara, op. cit., 152-200.

17. See O'Meara, 176-195.

18. See *Sacrae Theologiae Summa*, published by the Jesuit Professors in the various theological faculties in Spain (Madrid: La Editorial Católica, 1962) four volumes. These four volumes are a powerful and comprehensive statement of the post-Tridentine theology as it appeared from the seventeenth century down to the middle of the twentieth century. The amount of research which the various authors expended is in itself highly remarkable. These volumes present the over-riding theology of the Roman Catholic Church from 1650 to 1950. The theological movements just prior to Vatican II as well as the theology of the Vatican Council itself, plus the fifty years of post-Vatican II theology, has left the theology in these volumes "dated" and in many ways no longer applicable.

19. The appearance of Aristotle in the Western theological world began in the twelfth century, and it was almost immediately condemned by hierarchical church authority.

20. In the philosophy department at the University of Paris at the time of Albert and Thomas, there were some professors who found Aristotle's works all-inclusive. Revelation, in their view, was not needed. Neither Albert nor Thomas agreed with this approach to Aristotle. Rather, the philosophy of Aristotle which was inclusive of all created reality was seen as an area that could peacefully exist side-by-side with Christian faith. See O'Meara, op. cit., 13-14, 20-22, and 25-30.

21. To praise Thomism because of its Aristotelian framework does not mean that Thomism is the only way to bring philosophy and theology together. Nor can one say that Aristotle is the most important philosopher because he presented a unified form of metaphysics. Rather, I am saying only this: the ways in which Albert and Thomas united Christian faith to Aristotelian philosophy formed a unified theological tradition in an extraordinarily clear way. There are other equally clear systems of theology and philosophy which offer a different form of uniting religious thought to philosophical thought.

22. Over many centuries within the Western Catholic Tradition and even beyond, Thomism has been operative as a comprehensive program. However, there is not just one form of "Thomism." Rather, there are several forms of "Thomism," and all of these Thomistic forms have their own validity. However, each and every one of these forms is called "Thomism," because they are all established basically on Thomas' theology.

23. H. C, Lea, *A History of Auricular Confession and Indulgences in the Latin Church* (Philadelphia: Lea Brothers & Co, 1896).

24. See O'Meara, op. cit., "Aquinas, Theology, and Vatican II," 195-198; also "Beyond Vatican II," 198-200. O'Meara's last chapter, "Thomas Aquinas Today," 201-254, is a major attempt to bring aspects of Thomas' theology into the twenty-first century. O'Meara does this from his deep understanding of Thomas' theology, which in some ways can be disengaged from his Aristotelian philosophy.

25. See Thomas Nairn, ed., *The Franciscan Moral Vision: Responding to God's Love* (St. Bonaventure, NY: Franciscan Institute Publications, 2013), especially the two introductory essays by Kenan Osborne, "The Center of the Spiritual Vision of Francis and Clare: the Profound Relationship between God and Creation," 23-50, and "The Development of the Spiritual Vision of Francis and Clare into a Major Spiritual and Theological Tradition," 51-87.

26. See Théodore de Régnon, *Études de théologie positive sur la sainte Trinité*, 3. vols., (Paris: Victor Retaux et fils, 1892-1898). De Régnon's position on the scholastic teaching of the Trinity was maintained by A.

Stohr, M. Schmaus, F. Imle and J. Kaup, A. de Villamonte, and T. Szabo.

27. Zachary Hayes, "Introduction," in *Works of St. Bonaventure: Disputed Questions on the Mystery of the Trinity*, (St. Bonaventure, NY: The Franciscan Institute, 1979), 18. See the entire section from 13 to 24.

28. Olegario Gonzalez, *Misterio Trinitario y existencia humana: studio histórico teolgía en torno a San Buenaventura* (Madrid: Ediciones Rialp, 1965).

29. For a detailed description of Bonaventure's theology of Trinity, see K. Osborne, *A Theology of the Church for the Third Millennium: A Franciscan Approach*, 209-248; also Osborne, "The Trinity in Bonaventure," in *The Cambridge Companion to the Trinity*, ed. Peter Phan, (Cambridge: Cambridge University Press, 2011), 102-127.

30. See Johannes Freyer, *Homo Viator: Der Mensch im Lichte der Heilsgeschichte. Eine theologische Anthropologie aus franziskanischer Perspective* (Kevalaer: Verlag Butzon & Bercher, 2001), esp. 30-128.

31. Allan Wolter, "Duns Scotus and the Existence and Nature of God," reprinted from the *Proceedings of the American Catholic Philosophical Association*, (The Catholic University of America Press: Washington, D. C., 1954), 96.

32. Ibid. 96.

33. Scotus, *Ordinatio*, I d. 2, pars 1, qq. 1-2, n. 26, 138-139: The full Latin passage reads as follows: " Sed si quaeratur an esse insit alicui conceptui quem nos concipimus de Deo, ita quod talis proposito sit per se nota in qua enuntiatur esse de tali conceptu, puta de propositione cuius extrema possunt a nobis concipi, puta, potest in intellectu nostro esse aliquis conceptus dictus de Deo, tamen non communis sibi et creaturae, puta necessario esse vel ens infinitum vel summum bonum, et de tali conceptu possumus praedicare esse de eo modo quo a nobis concipitur, -- dico quod nulla talis est per se nota."

34. See Kenan Osborne and Ki Wook Min, *Science and Religion: Fifty Years after Vatican II*.

35. See Johannes Freyer, *Homo Viator: Der Mensch im Lichte der Heilsgeschichte*, 59-67, 91-96, 115-117.

36. See Freyer, op. cit., 91-96.

37. See Denzinger, op cit. ed., *Enchiridion Symbolorum, Definitionum, et Declarationum de Rebus Fidei et Morum*. Further references will read: *Denzinger,* followed by the paragraph number.

CHAPTER THREE

The History of Sacramental Theology From 1896 to 2014

The historical study of sacramental theology began in earnest sixty-six years before Vatican II. Consequently, many bishops at Vatican II were well aware of these historical studies even though the history of sacramental theology was not the main focus of the conciliar bishops. Rather, their main focus was to formulate an ecclesiology which was open to the contemporary world. To some extent, the historical details of the seven sacraments played a role in the pre-Vatican II renewal of ecclesiology, but the history of the sacraments was by no means center-stage during the conciliar discussions.

There are two major reasons why a chapter on the history of sacramental theology is of major importance for a study of ecclesiology fifty years after Vatican II. The first reason is this. The study of the history of the seven sacraments began in 1896 and has slowly become a major component for the study of sacramental theology. At first, the historical studies were seen as bothersome, since sacramental history challenged the standard approach to all seven sacraments. In 2014, the history of the seven sacraments remains somewhat at the edge of the theological mainstream of Catholic life, but its importance for sacramental theology cannot be set aside.In 1896 a protestant scholar, Henry Charles Lea, published a three-volume work entitled *A History of Auricular Confession and Indulgences in the Latin Church.*[1] Lea's book was a massive study, but it was also anti-Catholic. At the end of the nineteenth century, there were only a few Catholic scholars who were available to respond to Lea's work. A French canonist, August Boudinhon, was one of the first Catholics who replied to Lea's work, which he did in a lengthy article entitled "Sur l'histoire de la pénitence, à propos d'un livre récent."[2] As a scholar in canon law, Boudinhon was limited in his background regarding historical data on the sacraments; consequently, his negative complaints were focused more on the ways in which the sacramental history challenged the long-standing church laws regarding the sacrament of reconciliation.

At almost the same time that Boudinhon's article appeared, Francis Funk published an essay, "Zur altchrtistlichen Bussdisciplin."[3] Other essays began to appear that were written by competent scholars in church history. In 1902, for instance, Pierre Batiffol published a volume entitled, *Études d'histoire de théologie positive*[4] and P. A. Kirsch composed a book entitled *Zur Geschichte der katholischen Beichte.*[5] In 1903, Elphège Vacandard published *La penitence publique dans l'Église primitive.*[6] In 1906, F. Loofs, a Protestant scholar, published his volume, *Leitfaden zum Studium der Dogmengeschichte*, in which he sided more with the Catholic scholars than with Lea.[7]

Historical studies on the sacrament of reconciliation opened up an interest in historical studies regarding all seven sacraments. Carefully detailed publications on the histories of all the sacraments gradually appeared.

Scholars, such as Paul Galtier, Bernhard Poschmann, Adhémar D'Alès, Karl Adam, Josef Jungmann, Karl Rahner, Joseph Martos, and Dennis Petau turned their attention to publications on sacramental history. Their works continue to enrich our current understanding of each of the seven sacraments. However, a significant number of Catholic sacramental theologians seem to have ignored the historical data and continued to present sacramental theology in its Neo-Scholastic textbook form.[8]

The basic reason why many Catholic scholars hesitated to accept the historical material was the long-standing belief that Jesus Christ instituted the seven sacraments during his lifetime. Historical studies on the individual sacraments indicate that the sacraments of baptism and Eucharist had indeed been instituted by Jesus, but the other five sacraments seem to have been added later.

The second reason a chapter on the history of the sacraments is needed in this textbook is the book's focus on sacramental theology fifty years after the close of Vatican II. In these fifty years, the ecclesiology of the Catholic Church has also changed, which has affected the theology of sacraments. In other words, a theological change in ecclesiology has serious implications for the sacramental life of the Church. Post-Vatican II ecclesiology is more open to cultural issues and to the philosophies inherent in these non-Euro-American cultures. The ecclesial and sacramental openness to other cultures is not simply in language, music, and art; rather, these other cultures have a philosophical base which is expressed in language, music, art, etc. The question then arises: Are we able to express sacramental theology in and through the philosophical forms of non-Euro-American cultures?

The majority of bishops at Vatican II had a common task, namely, to develop an ecclesiology which was not oriented to the past but was instead open to current world situations. It is remarkable how much of the documentary material from Vatican II seriously opens the Catholic Church to the contemporary world. Vatican I was a council in which the bishops and the pope clung to the past; Vatican II was a council which opened doors and windows to the contemporary way of life. The bishops opened windows and doors and at times they even stepped beyond the doors and the windows. They saw the council as a time of new light, new air, and new views. They also realized that the three years of the council meetings provided insufficient time to develop the new openness of the Church, so they wanted post-conciliar scholars to use their insights and truly form an ecclesiology which speaks to today's world. In the fifty-years since Vatican II, Catholics have experienced the struggles to reform the church into an institution that is of service to the contemporary world.

Many changes in ecclesiology and in liturgy have occurred in today's Church as a result of sacramental history's proof that there have been many cultural adaptations over the Church's history. The Jesus-community was originally Jewish, but as time went on it separated from the Jewish community and moved into Greek and Latin communities. The philosophies of the Greek and Latin communities were not Jewish, so the explanation of the Christian faith came to be explicated in and through Greek and Latin philosophies. In the Eastern churches, the inculturation of the Christian Church became even more diverse, with a Syriac Church, a Coptic Church, an Armenian Church, etc.

Today, the Roman Catholic Church has opened itself to many cultures, each of which has its own philosophical base. The differing forms of contemporary sacramental life have attempted to accommodate sacramental liturgy to these various cultures, to new ways of understanding the world, and to new approaches to spirituality.

Chapter one presented the development of five different theological approaches to sacramental life that could not have occurred if there had not been a sense of freedom in sacramental life prior to Vatican II. The Neo-Scholastic theology of the seven sacraments had kept the Catholic Church within a single-way approach to sacramental life from the end of the Reformation down to the beginning of the twentieth century but historical studies on sacramental liturgy have opened the doors to new ways of thinking. The contemporary focus on the three Western theological traditions (chapter two) has also opened the doors to new ways of thinking as far as sacramental life is concerned, since contemporary Catholics are not restricted by a single theological tradition.

In order to assess these historical changes and to indicate their proper value for today's Catholic Church, chapter three is divided into four parts.

I. An Overview of the Development of the History of the Sacraments from 1896 to 2014

II. The References to the History of the Sacraments in the Documents of Vatican II

III. The References to the History of the Sacraments in the *Catechism of the Catholic Church*

IV. Conclusions

I. An Overview of the Development of the History of the Sacraments from 1896 to 2014

Henry Charles Lea's three-volume work on the sacrament of reconciliation was not the first attempt by theological scholars to formulate a history of the sacraments.[9] However, the publication of Lea's three volumes did enkindle far-reaching scholarly investigation of the history of all seven sacraments. This interest in the history of the sacraments continues to be alive and well. In the fifty years since Vatican II, the following volumes have been published by various theological and historical authors, each of whom was interested in sacramental history.

The History of the Sacrament of Baptism

AUTHOR	VOLUME
Edward Yarnold	*The Awe-Inspiring Rites of Initiation*, 1971.
Robert Hovda, ed.	*Made Not Born: New Perspectives on Christian Initiation and the Catechumenate*, 1976.
Michel Dujarier	*A History of the Catechumenate: The First Five Centuries*, 1978.
Aidan Kavanagh	*The Shape of Baptism: The Rite of Christian Initiation*, 1978.
E. C. Whitaker	*The Baptismal Liturgy*, 1981.
Adrian Nocent	*La Liturgia, I Sacramenti*, 1986.
Paul Bradshaw	*Essays in Early Eastern Initiation*, 1988.
Kilian McDonnell & George Montague	*Christian Initiation and Baptism in the Holy Spirit*, 1991.

The History of the Sacrament of the Eucharist

AUTHOR	VOLUME
Josef Jungmann	*Missarum sollemnia: eine genetische Erklärung der römischen Messe*, 1962.
Robert Daly	*The Origins of the Christian Doctrine of Sacrifice*, 1978.
Xavier Léon-Dufour	*Le Partage du Pain Eucharistique*, 1982.
Nathan Mitchell	*Cult and Controversy: The Worship of the Eucharist Outside of the Mass*, 1982.
Gary Macy	*The Theologies of the Eucharist in the Early Scholastic Period*, 1984.
David Power	*The Eucharistic Mystery*, 1989.
Gary Macy	*The Banquet's Wisdom, A Short History of the Theologies of the Lord's Supper*, 1992.

Similar listings could be made for the other five sacraments. I simply offer these titles as an indication that the study of the history of the sacraments has become a major part of today's study on sacramental theology.[10] These numerous studies on the history of each of the seven sacraments of the Catholic Church have raised issues which some church leaders find disturbing. Let us consider a few of these tender areas.

1. The history of the sacraments has raised a major question: Did Jesus institute all seven sacraments during his lifetime?

Today, this question has to be answered in a very careful manner, since the Council of Trent stated the issue in a tone of finality:

> Si quis dixerit, sacramenta novae Legis non fuisse omnia a Iesu Christo Domino nostro instituta … anathema sit.

> If anyone says that the sacraments of the new law were not all instituted by the Lord Jesus Christ … let that person be anathema.[11]

With this condemnation in mind, let us move carefully through the next few pages. In the opening chapter of this book, I referred to a four-volume theological work that was published by the faculty of the University of Salamanca in 1962, the very same year in which Vatican II began. In many ways, these four volumes contain the most thorough presentation of the Neo-Scholastic theology which had dominated the Catholic Church since the Reformation.

Joseph de Aldama was the author of large sections on sacramental theology, including the opening section, which is called "Theoria generalis sacramentorum"—"A general study of the sacraments." In his lengthy presentation, he cites statements from almost every scholar—Catholic, Eastern Church, and Protestant—who had written a serious document about the sacraments. Moreover, he cites almost every statement the Vatican Curia had made about the sacraments.

In chapter five of the text, Joseph de Aldama carefully nuances the statement on the institution of the sacrament. His thesis reads:

> "Christus, secundum quod homo, omnia sacramenta Novae Legis immediate instituit."

> "Christ, in his human nature, personally instituted all the sacraments of the New Law."[12]

He does not say that Jesus as God instituted the seven sacraments. Rather, he states that the human Jesus instituted the seven sacraments. He describes this institution as immediate, which in his explanation means that Jesus did not work through anyone else. Jesus, in his humanity, personally and directly established all seven sacraments. However, Aldama does say that Jesus left the task of determining the precise rituals to others, with the proviso that the rituals had to reflect the meaning and efficacy of each sacrament which Jesus himself had established.

However, when Aldama states his *"Nota Theologica"* for his thesis—a *nota theolgica* is the creedal value one places on a given theological position—he carefully modifies his position. A clear reading of his Latin text is of major importance:

> **Valor dogmaticus.** Institutio immediata omnium sacramentorum a Christo, videtur de fide divina et catholica definita; non tamen omnes theologi eodem modo loquuntur. Institutio a Christo secundum quod homo, est sententia communior et probabilior.

In English, we can translate the passage as follows:

> **Dogmatic value.** The immediate institution of all the sacraments by Christ seems to be a matter of divine faith which has been defined by the Catholic Church; but not all theologians speak in a unanimous way. The institution by Christ insofar as he is human is the more common and more probable opinion.

In many ways, one must have a strong grasp of Neo-Scholastic terminology to catch the innuendos and references in the above Latin statement. Aldama states that the institution of the seven sacraments is a matter of divine faith and it is a defined Catholic doctrine.

"Institutio immediate omnium sacramentorum a Christo, videtur de fide divina et catholica definita." Notice that he uses the term, "videtur" not "est."

He immediately adds that not all Catholic theologians agree with him. "Non omnes theologi eodem modo loquuntur."

Secondly, he states that "The institution by Christ as a human individual is a more common and more probable opinion." – "Institutio a Christ secundum quod homo est sententia communor et probabilior" (§141).

Aldama moves on to clarify his position in a roundabout way. He admits that the New Testament, in his view, has direct references to only four sacraments: baptism, Eucharist, penance, and holy orders. He says that the New Testament "does not teach an immediate [personal] institution of the other sacraments" (§142). He then adds that since Christ in his humanity was given universal power by God the Father, one is persuaded (*suadetur*) that all the sacraments were immediately instituted by Christ because of his universal power. Aldama then states that some of the early church fathers taught that Christ immediately instituted all of the Christian sacraments, citing Justin, Origen, Ephraem, Ambrose and Augustine. He adds that the medieval theologians also taught that Jesus instituted all seven sacraments.

Finally, Aldama speaks as a theologian, offering his own arguments. His first argument centers on the church. Jesus, he writes, instituted the church. However, since all seven sacraments are essential to the church, Jesus in instituting the church secondarily instituted the seven sacraments. Aldama's second argument centers on redemption in Christ. He argues that the institution of all seven sacraments is a major and essential part of the redemptive work of Jesus. If Jesus is the redeemer of the world, then he also instituted all seven sacraments because all seven sacraments are essential elements of Jesus' redemption (§144).

In a remarkable way, Aldama presents the Neo-Scholastic approach to the Christian sacraments in a thorough and well organized framework. Nonetheless, there are weaknesses to his position. First of all, the New Testament clearly states that baptism and Eucharist are central to the teaching of Jesus. His addition of reconciliation and holy orders does not have the same scriptural backing. In his citations of some Fathers of the Church, Aldama tends to read more into the text than they actually state. Thirdly, his final theological arguments are only as strong as their reasonability, and his argumentation does not seem to be conclusive.

I want to add a personal statement as well. I think Aldama has presented the Neo-Scholastic position in an excellent format. He cites any and all views and is careful in his wording. One quality shines out in his presentation, and that quality is thoroughness. Nonetheless, his presentation is one-sidedly Neo-Scholastic and not open to other views.

In the past fifty years, another issue apropos to the sacraments and to the Council of Trent has received attention.

2. A New Evaluation of the Tridentate Statement "*Anathema Sit*"

Thirty years before Vatican II, Catholic scholars began a slow but steady movement, namely a re-evaluation of the meaning of "*anathema sit*"—a person is anathematized. The rethinking of this phrase began in 1929 with some small articles, but in the 1940s and 1950s well documented works on the same issue appeared. In 1929, Johann Baptist Umberg published an article entitled "Die Bewertung der Trienter Lehren durch Pius VI" in which he compared the censures of Pius VI against the propositions of the Synod of Pistoia with the canons found in the decrees of Trent.[13] Umberg questioned whether the Synod of Pistoia dissented from Trent, and, if so, were these instances of dissent heretical. He concluded that there were only two instances in the propositions of the Synod of Pistoia that contradicted the censures of the Council of Trent, and the pope judged these two instances as heretical (anathematized). Umberg then examined the remaining proposals and concluded that the mere fact that something contradicted the canons of the Council of Trent did not, in itself, mean that the issue was heretical (anathematized).

In the same year, Heinrich Lennerz published an article, "Das Konzil von Trent und theologische Schulmeinungen," in which he noted that many penalties of Trent, even the penalty of *anathema sit*, should be considered *latae sententiae*, which means not in a strict fashion.[14]

In 1946 and 1947, R. Favre wrote a lengthy series of articles entitled "Les condemnations avec anathema,"[15] and in 1953, A. Lang published an article, "Die Bedeutungswandel der Bergriffe "fides" und "haeresis" und die dogmatische Wertung der Konzilsentscheidungen von Vienne und Trent."[16] Hubert Jedin, Piet Fransen, and Karl Peter have also contributed to this discussion on the theological value of the Tridentine statements on the sacraments and especially the phrase *anathema sit*.[17]

All of the above mentioned material indicates that Jesus did not institute all seven sacraments, and that there is nothing heretical about such a judgment. In the course of the history of the Church, rituals were established for reconciliation, anointing of the sick, ordination, confirmation, and marriage. At the end of the twelfth century, when Latin translations of almost all of Aristotle's writings had taken place, major theologians used the Aristotelian framework of essence and accident, causality, matter and form, minister and recipient as the framework for the scholastic explanation of sacramental theology. Thus, a non-religious philosophy was baptized into a Catholic format and the church slowly but surely was given the "Scholastic Theology of the Sacraments" and after the Reformation it was given the "Neo-Scholastic Theology of the Sacraments."

With all of the above in mind, let us reconsider the second reason for theological change. This was stated in the introduction of this chapter.

> A theological change in ecclesiology has serious implications for the sacramental life of the Church. Post-Vatican II ecclesiology is more open to cultural issues and to the philosophies inherent in these non-Euro-American cultures. The ecclesial and sacramental openness to other cultures is not simply in language, music, and art; rather, these other cultures have a philosophical base which is expressed in language, music, art, etc. The question then arises: Are we able to express sacramental theology in and through the philosophical forms of non-Euro-American cultures?

A culturally open ecclesiology clearly reaches to diverse languages, music, and art, but it also reaches out to the various cultural philosophies. Just as the Aristotelian philosophy entered into the sacramental theology at the end of the twelfth century and more deeply in the thirteenth and fourteenth centuries, so, too, one might surmise, today's Church leadership might reach out to the major cultures of the international world, specifically the philosophies in several major Asian cultures, major African cultures, and major Native cultures.

The Aristotelian philosophy is strongly centered on substance and accident. The Aristotelian meaning of the word substance (or essence) is: that which can be defined with no relationship to anything else. In the cultural philosophies mentioned in the preceding paragraph, relationship—not substance or essence—is at the heart of these cultural philosophies. Relationships are not static; rather, they are continually changing. A rethinking of sacramental theology might be seen as a mere de-Aristotelization of the theology, but Aristotelian philosophy has never been seen as a defined dogma of the church and therefore can be set to one side.

The new ecclesiology is also open to contemporary science, and two contemporary issues of today's scientific world are unabashedly relational. These two scientific dimensions are quantum mechanics and its descriptions of the microcosm, and the contemporary scientific age of the universe and its description of the macrocosm. We live in a relational universe and a non-relational philosophy no longer speaks to the world population in a fundamental way.

II. The References to the History of the Sacraments in the Documents of Vatican II

The Constitution on the Sacred Liturgy, *Sacrosanctum Concilium*, opened the door for liturgical change in a brief but important way. There is a clear reference to the opening of liturgy in the introduction of the document:

> Accordingly, it [the council] sees particularly cogent reasons
> for undertaking the reform and promotion of the liturgy.

The majority of bishops at Vatican II wanted to "reform" the liturgical celebrations of the church, particularly the sacramental celebrations and reform involves change. In the past fifty years, major liturgical changes have taken place, e.g., the vernacular celebration of the sacraments, the liturgical openness to diaconal and lay ministry, the role of women in sacramental celebrations, and to some extent, cultural changes in the celebration of the sacraments. Let us consider the changes mentioned in *Sacrosanctum Concilium*.

The Introductory Paragraphs of *Sacrosanctum Concilium*

In the introduction of *Sacrosanctum Concilium*, the bishops use the term renewal and advancement.

> That is why the sacred council judges that the following principles concerning the renewal and advancement of the liturgy should be called to mind and that practical norms should be established (§3).

The Latin text reads:

> Quare Sacrosanctum Concilium, de fovenda atque instauranda Liturgia quae sequuntur principia censet in mentem revocando et practicas normas stuatuendas esse.

In the English translation, two words focus on change: renewal and advancement. In the Latin text, the words are *principia* and *practicas normas*. The English words renewal and advancement overstep the Latin words *fovenda* and *instauranda* to some degree, but one can rightfully conclude that the conciliar bishops were stressing the need for change.

In the final paragraph of the introduction, the issue of liturgical change is stated in a clear and forthright way:

> The council also desires that, where necessary, the rites be revised carefully in the light of sound tradition, and that they [the rites] be given new vigor to meet present-day circumstances and need (§4).

The Latin reads:

> Sacrosanctum Concilium ... atque optat ut, ubi opus sit, caute ex integro ad mentem sanae traditionis recognoscantur de novo vigore, pro hodernis adiunctis et necssitatibus, donentur.

In this paragraph, the bishops clearly state that a revision of the sacramental rites should take place so as to give a new impetus to present-day circumstances. The door for change is open, and change should take place in a careful way.

Chapter One of *Sacrosanctum Concilium*

In chapter one of *Sacrosanctum Concilium*, the bishops focus on baptism and Eucharist in the early apostolic church (§§5-6). They then move on to sacramental life in general and state "that when anybody baptizes, it is really Christ himself who baptizes" (§7).

This description of baptism is not quite the same as the wording in the *Catechism* on the *Christus totus,* but the words move us to a similar understanding of who baptizes, who confirms, who celebrates the Eucharist, etc. The English text of *Sacrosanctum Concilium* reads:

> It follows that every liturgical celebration, because it is an action of Christ the priest and of his body, which is the church, is preeminently sacred action" (§7).

The Latin text reads:

> Proinde omnis liturgica celebratio, utpote opus Christi sacerdotis eiusque Corporis, quod est Eccelesia, est actio sacra praecellenter.

In these words, the *Catechism's* phrase of *Christus totus* is clearly evident in the conciliar document. This phrase means that "It is the whole community, the Body of Christ united with his Head, that celebrates" (*Catechism*, §§1136 and 1140).

In Chapter I of *Sacrosanctum Concilium*, §11 we read:

> Priestly pastors must also ensure that the faithful take part fully aware of what they are doing, actively engaged in the rite and enriched by it.

The Latin text reads:

> Ideo sacris pastoribus ad vigilandum est ut in actione liturgica non solum observentur leges ad validam et licitam celebrationem, sed ut fideles scienter, actuose et fructuose eandem participant.

In some parish churches, the celebrant is very careful to follow the liturgical norms and regulations. The bishops, in this statement, are saying that the celebrant should also ensure that the faithful are know-ingly, actively, and effectively present (*scienter, actuose, et fructuose*). The barrier between the priest at the altar and the people in the pews should be reduced as much as possible. This greater involvement of the people in liturgical celebrations is clearly a change from the way the Mass was most often celebrated prior to Vatican II.

In a latter section of *Sacrosanctum Concilium*, the bishops focus on the liturgical training of seminarians (§§15, 16, and 17). They state that in theological faculties, liturgy is to be one of the principal courses. "It is to be taught under its theological, historical, spiritual, pastoral and juridical aspects" (§16). The Latin text reads: "Disciplina de sa-cra Liturgia in seminariis et studiorum domibus religiosis ... sub as-pectu cum theologico et historico, tum spirituali, pastorali et iuridico tradenda." The word historical means that the history of the seven sacraments should be an integral part of the course on liturgy that all seminarians must take.

In §21, the bishops again state that the Church should undertake a careful general reform of the liturgy. The bishops are clearly opposed to any careless reform.

In many ways, the most radical statement of the bishops is found in the "Norms for Adapting the Liturgy to the Temperament and Tra-ditions of Peoples" §§37-40. In the opening sentence, the bishops state that they do not wish to impose a rigid uniformity in matters which do not affect the faith of the well-being of the entire community." The bishops focus on the qualities and talents of various races and nations. The issue of acculturation of liturgy is stated in a clear way:

> Anything in people's way of life which is not indissolubly bound up with superstition and error the church studies with sympathy, and, if possible, preserves intact. It sometimes even admits such things into the liturgy itself, provided they

harmonize with its true and authentic spirit" (§37).

The local bishops are singled out as the leadership that can allow cultural adaptations. These adaptations include processions, liturgical language, sacred music, and art. As long as these adaptations conform to the norms laid down in *Sacrosanctum Concilium*, the local bishops are seen as the leaders in the cultural adaptation process (§39).

One of the most striking statements in the conciliar regulations involves "radical" changes. The bishops carefully word this statement. It is a lengthy statement, so I offer only the English text:

> In some places and circumstances, however, an even more radical adaptation of the liturgy is needed and this entails greater difficulties. For this reason: (1) The competent territorial ecclesiastical authority mentioned in article 22.2 must, in this matter, carefully and prudently consider which elements form the traditions and cultures of individual peoples might appropriately be admitted into divine worship. Adaptations which are considered useful or necessary should then be submitted to the Apostolic See to be introduced with its consent. (2) To ensure that adaptations may be made with the requisite care, the Apostolic See will, if needs be, grant permission to this same territorial ecclesiastical authority to permit and to direct the necessary preliminary experiments over a period of time among certain groups suitable for the purpose. (3) Because liturgical laws usually involve special difficulties with respect to adaptation, especially in mission lands, people who are experts in the matters in question must be employed when they are formulated (§40).

The use of the term radical is important. In Latin, the text reads: "Cum tamen variis in locis et adiunctis, profundior Liturgiae aptatio urgeat, et ideo difficilior evadat." The English translation is "more radical" and the Latin original is *profundior*—more profound.

Whether *profundior* translates into more radical or more profound is a textual matter. What should be noted here is the openness of the bishops to major changes. Even more important is the fact that the conciliar bishops, in these regulations, opened the church to a multi-cultural world and basically asked for a better integration of liturgy into the multi-cultural world.

Prior to Vatican II, missionaries from the Euro-American arena went to areas in which the culture and the philosophy were entirely different. Their mandate was to Christianize the people in these areas, but they were to do so by implanting Euro-American forms of liturgy into a foreign country. In this section of the Constitution on the Liturgy, the Catholic leaders are called on to integrate the cultural aspects of a given society into the liturgical celebration in more radical or more profound ways.

The changes in the liturgy were established in *Sacrosanctum Concilium* in 1963. From 1963 to 2014, liturgical adaptations have certainly taken place, but radical liturgical adaptations have faced strong opposition by the Apostolic See. The conservative element in the leadership of the Church has timidly opted for radical cultural changes in the liturgy.

In local areas of the multi-cultural world, radical liturgical changes have been made even without official sanction of the Apostolic See. This is not new for liturgical celebrations. In the early centuries of the Church, the sacrament of reconciliation was a public event and was for adults only. Gradually, but with strong opposition from the Roman world, a Celtic form of reconciliation, which was private and available to all, became the acceptable form of reconciliation that we experience even today. Additionally, the celebration of marriage took place in the early centuries in ways which local societies had approved. The requirement that marriage take place within a priestly-guided liturgy did not become standard until the twelfth century. There are many other examples in which a local population followed its own trends and only later did Rome impose a unified liturgical celebration.

Sacrosanctum Concilium opened doors and windows for liturgical renewal and major liturgical renewals have taken place because of the bishops' efforts. However, John Paul II and Benedict XVI wanted the Catholic Church to be a highly unified church, so the resulting changes in the officially approved liturgy were not radical. In one of his addresses to the bishops of Africa, Paul VI mentioned that he hoped that one day there might be an "eglise africaine." John Paul II, on several occasions cited the talk by Paul VI, but never used the sentence that included the phrase "eglise africaine." John Paul II wanted only an "eglise catholique," one church for the whole world, no matter what the cultural factors might be.

III. The References to the History of the Sacraments in the Catechism of the Catholic Church

As mentioned in chapter one, the *Catechism of the Catholic Church* presents very limited views of the historical development of the seven sacramental rituals and their theology. The explanation of the sacraments in Section Two of the *Catechism* focuses almost exclusively on the sacramental life in today's church, by-passing the historical developments of the sacramental rituals. Let us consider how the *Catechism* presents the historical material on each sacrament.

Baptism and Confirmation

For baptism, there is only one brief paragraph (§1230) that refers to the historical development of baptism. Since it is printed in smaller type, the data is of secondary value (see §20). For confirmation, there are two paragraphs, §§ 1290 and 1291, which refer to the historical development and theology of confirmation, and these references are also in small print.

Eucharist

For the Eucharist, the authors of the *Catechism* mention at length the historical writings of Justin. The authors state why this is included in the *Catechism*:

> As early as the second century we have the witness of St. Justin Martyr for the basic lines of the order of the Eucharistic celebration. They have stayed the same until our own day for the great liturgical families (§1345).

The way in which Justin describes the Eucharistic celebration is referred to as an unchanged format down to the present time. In other words, the authors of the *Catechism* felt that the format of the Eucharist had not experienced any historical changes. However, the Eucharistic celebration has actually had many changes from the time of Justin down to the present, and today's Eucharistic liturgies in the Eastern Churches are significantly different from the Eucharistic liturgies in the Western Churches.

In the Catechism §1356, we read: "If from the beginning Christians have celebrated Eucharist and in a form whose substance has not changed despite the great diversity and liturgies, it is because we know ourselves to be bound by the command the Lord gave on the eve of his Passion: 'Do this in remembrance of me.'" This conclusion is questionable, since the terminology is Aristotelian and the philosophical background is also Aristotelian. The term "substance" is used by the authors of the *Catechism* to explain that the liturgy at the time of Justin was the same as it is today. In other words, Aristotle's philosophy is being used by the authors of the *Catechism* to explain Justin's presentation of the Eucharist.[18]

From Justin's *First Apology*, written around 150 C.E., we have a detailed description of a Eucharistic celebration that took place after the baptism of a catechumen. This description offers us a glimpse of a Eucharistic celebration in Rome in the middle of the second century. M. Jourjon, in his section on Justin in *The Eucharist of the Early Christians*, states four main issues for the Eucharistic assembly in Justin's presentation. First of all, it took place "on the day named after the sun." Secondly, Justin makes a clear distinction between presider and people. Thirdly, Justin mentions "deacons" who "summon each one present to partake of the bread and wine and water over which the thanksgiving was made and they [deacons] carry it also to those who are absent." Jourjon notes that "water" is presented, since the custom was to dilute the wine a person was drinking. Fourthly, in a way similar to the *Didache*, there is in Justin's essay a "prayer of praise for blessings received." In the Eucharistic prayer of Justin, the words of institution—"this is my body and this is my blood"—are not included. The words of institution are also not included in the *Didache*. The Eucharistic prayer in Justin's Apology is simply a prayer of thanksgiving.[19] Today, if a priest does not say the words of institution, most Catholic theologians would say that the Mass was invalid.

We see changes in the Eucharistic Liturgy as early as Justin's time, but the major change in that time period was the cessation of a meal in which the Eucharistic bread was celebrated at the beginning of the meal and the Eucharistic wine was celebrated at the end of the meal. A major reason for eliminating the meal was the growing number of baptized participants.[20]

Likewise, in a later century, the words of institution—"this is my body and this is my blood"—became central to the Eucharistic prayer. The authors of the *Catechism* do indeed state that "the basic lines of the order of the Eucharistic celebration [in Justin's Apology] have stayed the same until our own day," but this is neither historically or theologically accurate. The pre Vatican II Eucharistic theology of the Catholic Church emphasized the words of institution, and these words of institution were central to the celebration of Eucharist.

Reconciliation

In §1447, the authors of the *Catechism* offer a lengthy paragraph on the historical changes in the liturgical celebration of the sacrament of penance. Chapter one of this text mentioned that the public form of penance, which was normative in the early centuries of the church, was challenged from the seventh century onward by the private form of penance derived from the Celtic missionaries. The *Catechism* does not mention the rancor and condemnation of the Celtic form of penance by the Roman Church. In the Roman world at that time, Christians who did not commit a few specifically-named grave sins, such as publicly known murder, adultery, and denial of the Catholic faith, continued to attend Eucharist and receive Holy Communion. At this early time, the Roman Church considered Eucharist to be a sacrament of reconciliation for all sins except those which were considered heinous, specifically those mentioned above. A majority of ordinary Christians never received the sacrament of reconciliation during his or her entire life, but they did receive communion whenever they attended the Eucharistic liturgy.

The dispute between the Roman form of reconciliation and the Celtic form of reconciliation, however, began to raise questions regarding Christians who sinned seriously from today's standpoint but who were never sacramentally reconciled during the first eight or nine centuries. These "sinners" did receive communion at Mass and the Eucharist itself was reconciling. Gradually, the Celtic form of penance became standard throughout Europe. Only in 1215, at the fourth Lateran Council, did the Roman Church officially endorse the Celtic form of penance as the standard form for reconciliation. The Roman Church bishops did this indirectly, for their statement reads:

> Let everyone of the faithful of either sex, after reaching the age of discretion, faithfully confess in secret to his own priest all his sins, at least once a year, and diligently strive to fulfill the penance imposed on him.[21]

Nowhere does this conciliar document state that a change in the sacrament of reconciliation has taken place. Rather, it simply endorses the Celtic form of penance in an indirect way. Public penance lingered on for a short time afterwards, but by the end of the 13th century it had disappeared altogether, except in extenuating circumstances such as absolving a group of soldiers who were moving into battle.

Anointing of the Sick

In the *Catechism* §1512, there is a brief overview of the anointing of the sick. The *Catechism* does not mention any of the radical changes of this sacrament. At first, oil was blessed during the Sunday liturgy and the vials of oil were taken home by women and men and used abundantly by the laity. A radical change, however, took place during the Carolingian Reformation, from the ninth to the eleventh century, when slowly but surely the anointing of the sick began to be disallowed by lay men and women. The anointing of the sick was restricted to the priest since theological development was gradually changed in the Carolingian Reform. The anointing of the sick as a liturgical act became a ritual in which sin was forgiven. Forgiveness of sin, of course, could only be done by a priest or bishop. One can only say that the sacrament of anointing of the sick was radically changed during the Carolingian Reform and that church leadership validated this change by restricting anointing of the sick to an ordained priestly minister.

Holy Orders

Article 6 of the *Catechism* (§§1536-1600) deals with the sacrament of holy orders. In this section of the *Catechism*, the Roman priest, Hippolytus (ca. 170-236), is quoted twice. In his extant writings, we have the first historical text of an ordination of bishop, priest and deacon. Hippolytus' work dates from the beginning of the third century. Prior to this time, we have no idea how one was selected to be a bishop, priest, or deacon or how one might have been ordained to holy orders. After the above third-century liturgical text of Hippolytus, no mention of this document is found anywhere for another hundred years. Since it was a document used in Rome, one could easily ask whether the ordination ritual had any influence outside of Rome. For one hundred years, there is only silence on this subject. A century later, one finds parts of the document in the northern Gallic sphere of Europe. From then on, we have traces of a sacramental rite for ordination leading to an eventual full-rite of ordination.

Historically, we have no clear idea how a person might have been selected as a priest, bishop, or deacon, prior to the rituals of Hippolytus. Consequently, to speak of a sacramental matter, form, minister and recipient prior to 200 C.E. is questionable. From 300 C.E. onward, there are instances of an ordination in many European areas, and some of these ordination rituals became standard both in the Western Catholic Church and in the Eastern Catholic Churches. All of this raises the question: did Jesus ordain his major disciples? Was there an ordination to episcopacy, priesthood, and diaconate prior to 200 C.E.? If the answer to these questions is no, then the sacrament of ordination was not instituted by Christ during his lifetime.[22]

In the *Catechism*, §1536, the authors state the following:

> On the institution and the mission of the apostolic ministry
> by Christ, see above no. 874 ff. Here [the section on the sacra-
> ment of Holy Orders] only the sacramental means by which
> this ministry is handed on will be treated."

When we turn to §§874-896, the authors of that section focus on
the hierarchical constitution of the church. In these pages, it is simply asserted that the holy orders of priesthood and episcopacy were
instituted by Jesus during his life and that the specific duties of sacramental rituals, the ministry of teaching, and the ministry of govern-
ing of pope, bishop, and priest were all clearly established during the
lifetime of Jesus. No mention, not even in the footnotes, is made that
these conclusions have been questioned by contemporary scriptural
scholars, church historians, and systematic theologians.[23] Many capa-
ble contemporary Catholic scholars have questioned the suggestion
that Jesus instituted the sacrament of holy orders during his lifetime.

The sacraments of baptism and Eucharist are clearly stated in the
New Testament material; the other five sacraments are not presented
in the New Testament as sacraments. References to an anointing of the
sick, a forgiveness of sin, marriage, gospel ministry, and the presence
of the Holy Spirit are all found in the New Testament, but these references are at times generalized. It is questionable whether there were
sacramental structures for these five religious actions. In spite of this,
the *Catechism* tends to avoid historical questioning whether Jesus instituted all seven sacraments.

Matrimony

The historical material on the sacrament of matrimony is not very
clear in the *Catechism* (§§1601-1666). The authors begin with an over-

view of marriage as a human form of life. They stress that marriage was and remains a part of God's plan for all humanity: "The intimate community of life and love which constitutes the married state has been established by Creator and endowed by him with its own proper laws ... God himself is the author of marriage."[24] None of this centers on the sacramentality of marriage; it centers on the fact that from the beginning men and women have married.

The authors then move into marriage in the Jewish world prior to Jesus. In this period of time, Moses permitted men to divorce their wives and in the Old Testament, the polygamy of patriarchs and kings is not explicitly rejected.

When the authors move to the New Testament, they focus on the marriage feast in the town of Cana. Jesus' presence is described as follows:

> The Church attaches great importance to Jesus' presence at the wedding at Cana. She sees in it the confirmation of the goodness of marriage and the proclamation that thenceforth marriage will be an efficacious sign of Christ's presence (§1613).

In the theological textbooks prior to Vatican II, the sacramentality of marriage is not argued from the wedding feast at Cana. Rather, the arguments are based on Matthew 19:9, "Whoever divorces his wife and marries commits adultery," and the Letter to the Ephesians 5:22-32. Some of these textbooks mention that later Fathers of the Church, such as Epiphanius and Augustine, did refer to the wedding feast at Cana but these authors did not state that marriage became a sacrament at Cana.[25]

At the Second Council of Lyons in 1274, Pope Gregory X required the Emperor, Michael Palaeologus, to make a profession of faith in which there was an enumeration of the seven sacraments, including marriage. This is the first high-ranking papal statement on the seven sacraments. Given all of the above information on marriage, one can conclude that in the history of the sacrament of marriage, there are major historical issues in the *Catechism* which are not adequately developed.

Part three of this present chapter is entitled "The References to the History of the Sacraments in the *Catechism of the Catholic Church*." Unfortunately, the authors of the *Catechism* tended to avoid the historical data that scholars have brought to light in great detail over the past century as regards each of the seven sacraments. The few historical references made by the authors in this section of the *Catechism* indicate that they were aware of the historical work of sacramental scholars; however, the authors tended to remain within the pre-Vatican II Neo-Scholastic framework of sacramental theology.

IV. Conclusions

The ordinary Catholic reader of the *Catechism* probably still believes that Jesus instituted all seven sacraments.[26] On the basis of the history of each sacrament, however, I believe that I can make the following conclusions.

1. In the official statements of the Church, such as the documents of Vatican II and the *Catechism of the Catholic Church*, little to no attention has been given to the history of the seven sacraments and the implications that this history indicates.

In the documents of Vatican II, one would not expect to find detailed references to the history of the sacraments. The conciliar bishops had one major focus: to present a theology of church that was open to today's world. They did not want to repeat a theology of church focused on the Reformation or on the nineteenth century secularization (Vatican I). The bishops were clearly centered on today's issues and on the ways in which the Catholic Church might be of some assistance. Neither the specific sacraments nor their specific history were of major concern for the conciliar bishops.

The goals of the *Catechism of the Catholic Church* are not the same as the goals of the bishops at Vatican II. The authors of the *Catechism*—all anonymous—were commissioned by Pope John Paul II to present "a statement of the Church's faith and of catholic doctrine attested to or illuminated by Sacred Scripture, the Apostolic Tradition, and the Church's Magisterium."[27]

In Part Two, Section Two of the *Catechism of the Catholic Church*, the authors provide an overview of the theology of the seven sacraments. The first sentence of the opening paragraph indicates what this lengthy section is all about:

> Christ instituted the sacraments of the new law. There are seven: Baptism, Confirmation (or Chrismation), the Eucharist, Penance, the Anointing of the Sick, Holy Orders, and Matrimony (§1210).

The authors of this section of the *Catechism* make a clear statement that Christ instituted the sacraments and that there are seven sacraments in the Catholic Church. Prior to Vatican II, many Catholics had memorized a similar form of this statement when, as children, they were instructed in Catholic teaching through the *Baltimore Catechism*. Up to 1950, almost all Catholics followed the belief that Jesus had instituted the seven sacraments during his life on earth.

Nonetheless, the historical studies on the sacraments have changed the theology of the sacraments in a profound way. In the New Testament, the ritual of baptism is clearly described in the activity of John the Baptist, and especially in his baptism of Jesus. Baptism is frequently mentioned in the letters of St. Paul and in the Acts of the Apostles.[28] However, the possible subjects of baptism and the effects of baptism have been expressed in different way over the past 1,900 years.[29] Before the time of Augustine (354-430), original sin had not yet been incorporated into baptismal theology. Today, in the RCIA, which is a lengthy spiritual journey for someone who wishes to become Catholic, the actual baptism, confirmation, and first Eucharist are by no means a time when the individual receives grace or is forgiven original sin. In his or her RCIA journey, sanctifying grace has already been received, and the person has spiritually accepted Catholic faith. All of these are already present in an RCIA member when he or she is baptized, confirmed and receives first Eucharist. Consequently, a major question arises: what is being celebrated in the final stage of the RCIA? I would suggest that we are celebrating what God has done, is doing, and— we pray—continues to do in the life of this woman or man. In other words, the conferral of something new is not present when a member of the RCIA first receives baptism, confirmation, and first Eucharist.

The Eucharist is also mentioned in the New Testament, especially in the descriptions of the Last Supper that are found in all four gospels. Moreover, Paul's letters, the Acts of the Apostles, and John's letters all refer to the Eucharist.[30] These passages have guided church communities in the structuring of the liturgical actions. However, there is no single form of liturgy for the celebration of the Eucharist, as the history of this sacrament makes clear. Even today there are wide differences between the Roman Catholic liturgical celebration of the Eucharist and the liturgical celebration of Eucharist in the Eastern Rites. Moreover, between East and West, Eucharistic theology moves in differing directions. The Eastern and Western Eucharistic rituals and the Eucharistic theologies behind them have not remained the same over the centuries.

The history of the sacrament of reconciliation has changed many times over the centuries. In the New Testament, forgiveness of sin is a central message. Jesus often says "Go and sin no more." However, it is the well-known passages in Matthew 16:16 and 18:18, and in John 20:22-23 that theologians have used to established Jesus' institution of the sacrament of penance: "Whose sins you shall forgive shall be forgiven and whose sins you shall retain, shall be retained."[31]

In the post-apostolic age up to Hermas (c. 140), we have no historical data about a ritualized practice of reconciliation. The *Didache*, Clement of Rome's Letter to the Corinthians, the letters of Ignatius of Antioch, the writings of Polycarp of Smyrna, the *Epistula Apostolorum* and the Epistle of Barnabas offer nothing on the theme of the Church's ritualized penitential practices of that time. All of these writings, however, mention, in some fashion or another, the forgiveness of God that Jesus has brought to us. There is a power in the church to repel, isolate and negate sin; it has been and still is today apparent in many ways beyond the sacrament of penance. Here and there, we find clear indications of serious post-baptismal sins, but we have no clue regarding a ritual of reconciliation. Emmanuel Bourke, together with many others, notes that in the sub-apostolic period there was a general tendency towards rigorism so that, once baptized, the Christian was seen as someone who ought never sin again. This rigorism helps to explain some of the difficulties the early patristic church encountered in their efforts to apply the power to forgive serious post-baptismal sin.[32]

In the writings of Tertullian (c. 150-230), there are only generic references to a penitential ritual after baptism, which include no clear details of a ritual and its regulations about who are eligible for a public reconciliation. The same conclusion can be drawn from the writings of Clement of Alexandria (c. 150-215), in which reconciliation is mentioned but no ritual is described. In his later writings, Origen (c. 185-254) indicates some sins could not even be forgiven by a penitential service. The *Shepherd of Hermas*, written in mid-second century, mentions a ritual but offers no clear description of the ritual.[33]

In all of this early history on reconciliation, a ritual of reconciliation does not stand out as "the" way in which a Christian sinner is brought back into the community. It is one thing to talk about reconciliation, but it is quite another thing to talk about a ritual of reconciliation. The ritualized format of reconciliation seems to have been developed in the late second century, thus a ritualized form of reconciliation that is a sacramental form of reconciliation did not originate with Jesus. Rather, it is a creation of the Jesus community more than one hundred years after the death and resurrection of Jesus. The other sacraments have similar histories that call into question their institution by Jesus.

The position on the seven sacraments as stated in the *Catechism* does not present a full understanding of sacramental theology. Rather, it is in many ways simply a repeat of pre-Vatican II sacramental theology.

2. In the *Catechism*, Part Two is dedicated to the liturgical celebration of the Christian mystery. Part Two is divided into two sections. Section One is entitled the Sacramental Economy and Section Two is entitled The Seven Sacraments of the Church. My conclusion is that each section has its own "theology of sacraments" and that the two theologies are worlds apart.

Since many authors contributed to the essays in the *Catechism*, one cannot expect uniformity. However, the two sections on the sacraments were meant to contribute to each other as stated in the introductory passage §1076. It is my conclusion that Section One presents a very exciting theology of the sacraments based on the Trinitarian God, on the *Christus totus*, and on Jesus as the *Lumen Gentium*. This focus, however, is not the focus of Section Two, which as stated above is a restatement of pre-Vatican II sacramental theology. The two sections seem to move in different directions.

The new focus on the Trinity, on *Christus totus*, and on the meaning of *Lumen Gentium* is, in my judgment, a remarkable beginning of a sacramental theology which will speak to the Catholic community today. It will also be a sacramental theology that will be of tremendous value for the ecumenical discussions that are a major part of today's ecclesiology. This Trinitarian form of sacramental theology will also help the Church's current efforts to incorporate cultural aspects into sacramental celebrations. Finally, in my view, the Trinitarian form of sacramental theology can also be of service to inter-religion conversations that are an inevitable part of the Church in the twenty-first century.

Endnotes

1. See Lea, *A History of Auricular Confession and Indulgences in the Latin Church*.

2. August Boudinhon, "Sur l'histoire de la penitence, à propos d'un livre récent." *Revue d'histoire et de literature religieuse*, 2 (1897), 306-344 and 496-524.

3. Francis X. Funk, "Zur altchristlichen Bussdisciplin," *Kirchengeschichtliche Abhandlungen und Untersuchungen*, v. 1 (Paderborn: F. Schoningh, 1896), 155-209.

4. Pierre Battifol, *Études d'histoire et de théologie positive* (Paris: V. Lecoffre, 1902).

5. P. A. Kirsch, *Zur Geschichte der katholischen Beichte* (Würzburg: Gobel und Scherer, 1902).

6. Elphège. F. Vacandard, *La penitence publique dans l'Église primitive* (Paris: Bloud, 1903).

7. F. Loofs, *Leitfaden zum Studium der Dogmengeschichte* (Leipzig: Halle Niemeier, 1906).

8. Professors such as Gartmeier in Germany and Pignataro and Di Dario in Italy wrote monographs in which egregious historical errors were put forward as truth and this was done, in their view, as a defense of the status quo. See Kenan Osborne, *Sacramental Theology*, 2-10.

9. Prior to Lea, scholars in the nineteenth century had called for a new form of ecclesiology, and this new form included a reconstruction of the sacramental system. See material on Johann Sebastian Drey (1777-1853 and Johann Adam Möhler (1796-1838).

10. For the history of the other five sacraments, see the detailed bibliography in my volume, *Christian Sacraments in a Postmodern World* (New York: Paulist Press, 1999), 200-202.

11. *Denzinger*, n. 1601.

12. Joseph de Aldama, "Tractatus I: Theoria generalis sacramentorum," *Sacrae Theologiae Summa*, IV, 96.

13. Johann Baptist Umberg, "Die Bewertung der Trienter Lehren durch Pius VI," in *Scholastik*, 4 (1929), 402-409.

14. Heinrich Lennerz, "Das Konzil von Trient und theologische Schulmeinungen," in *Scholastik*, 4 (1929). 38-53. Lennerz wrote a subsequent article, "Notulae Tridentinae, Primum Anathema in Concilio Tridentino," in *Gregorianum* 27 (1946), 136-142.

15. R. Favre, "Les condemnations avec anathema," *Bulletin de Literature Écclésiastique*, 17 (1946), 226-241 and 18 (1947), 31-48.

16. A Lang, "Die Bedeutungswandel der Begriffe "fides" und "haeresis" und die dogmatische Wertung der Konzilsentscheidungen von Vienne und Trent," *Münchener Theologische Zeitschrift*, 4 (1953), 133-156.

17. See Hubert Jedin, *A History of the Council of Trent*, Eng. trans. by E. Graf (St. Louis, MO: B. Herder Book Co., 1961); Piet Fransen, "Réflexions sur l'anathème au Concile de Trente," *Ephemerides théologiques lovanienses*, 29 (1953); Carl J. Peter, "Auricular Confession and the Council of Trent," *The Jurist*, (1968).

18. See CCC, n. 902.

19. See M. Jourjon, "Justin," in *The Eucharist of the Early Church*, Willy Rodorf, ed., (New York: Pueblo Publishing Co., 1978), 71-85; in this same volume, W. Rodorf wrote a chapter on "The Didache," 1-23. Edward Kilmaratin has also written in detail on early Christian eucharist including the Eucharistic passages in Justin: see *The Eucharist in the Primitive Church* (Englewoood Cliffs, NJ: Prentice Hall, 1965), 148-150. His material on Justin is detailed and twice he mentions that the service was based on a Jewish synagogue ritual. Kilmartin notes that Justin's form of eucharist influenced the area around Rome. See also Robert Cabié, *Histoire de la Messe* (Paris: Desclée, 1990); Eng. trans. by Lawrence Johnson, *History of the Mass* (Washington, DC: The Pastoral Press, 1992).

20. See Kilmartin, op. cit., 149-150.

21. See *Denzinger*, n. 221.

22. For a detailed book on the ordination of bishops, see Sharon McMillen, *Episcopal Ordination and Ecclesial Consensus*, (Collegeville, MN: Liturgical Press, 2005).

23. For a general explanation of the "institution" of Holy Orders, see Frederick Cwiekowski, "Holy Orders," *The Harpercollins Encyclopedia of Catholicism*, 620-625. See also, Bernard Cooke, *Ministry to Word and Sacraments: History and Theology* (Philadelphia: Fortress Press, 1976); Thomas F. O'Meara, *Theology of Ministry* (New York: Paulist Press, 1983); David Power, *Ministers of Christ and His Church: Theology of Priesthood* (London: Geoffrey Chapman, 1969); and Kenan Osborne, *Priesthood: A History of Ordained Priesthood in the Roman Catholic Church* (New York: Paulist Press, 1989).

24. The editors of the CCC are quoting from the Vatican II document, *Gaudium et Spes*, n. 48, 1.

25. See Francisco, Solá, "De Matrimonio," *Sacrae Theologiae Summa*, pp. 691-824, esp. 731-732.

26. The issue of the institution of the sacraments by Jesus is simply one instance among many, in which the *Catechism* takes a stand without any indication that there are other views. The major failure of the CCC is the fact that the authors rarely mention if the position under consideration is a defined matter of faith, or a position which at this period of time is the official church stance and which can be changed, or finally which positions are simply the views of theologians such as Thomas Aquinas. Secondly, the *CCC*, in certain dioceses, has been presented as the correct explanation of Catholic teaching. Such a judgment is substantiated by the two introductory statements of John Paul II, who describes the *CCC* as a "genuine, systematic presentation of the faith and of Catholic doctrine a totally reliable way to present, with renewed fervor, each and every part of the Christian message to the people of our time" (*Magnopere*, p. xv). He also wrote: "The *Catechism of the Catholic Church* ...is a statement of the Church's faith and of catholic doctrine, attested to or illumined by Sacred Scripture, the Apostolic Tradition, and the Church's Magisterium. (*Fidei Depositum*, p. 5). The *CCC*, in reality, *offers* only "one view" of Catholic Teaching.

27. See John Paul II, Apostolic Constitution, *Fidei Depositum*, which is one of the opening papal statements of the CCC, page 5.

28. See, Kenan Osborne, *The Christian Sacraments of Initiation: Baptism, Confirmation, Eucharist* (Mahwah, NJ: Paulist Press, 1987), 5-104.

29. An example of this is the baptism of infants. In the early centuries of the Church, infants and children were not baptized. Even Augustine in the fifth century could not give a satisfactory answer to the issue

of infant/child death, since at that time infants and children were not baptized.

30. Osborne, op. cit., 141-233.

31. See Kenan Osborne, *Reconciliation and Justification: The Sacrament and Its Theology*, 17-24.

32. See Emmanuel Bourque, *Histoire de la Pénitence-Sacrement* (Quebec: Laval University Press, 1947), 63-65.

33. See Osborne, *Reconciliation and Justification*, 52-74.

CHAPTER FOUR

The Liturgy – Work of the Holy Spirit

In the first three chapters, we saw that five different theologies of the sacraments become well-known within the Catholic Church in the years just prior to Vatican II and during the fifty years afterwards. Many professors and many catechists have used the material in these five forms of sacraments in one way or another.

Individual Catholic theologians have also written articles and books which present a theology of sacraments different, at least to some degree, from the five mentioned above. These sacramental theologies are important since they show that there has been a continuing reflection on Catholic sacramental life. However, for the most part these individual views have remained limited in their influence and thus their approaches to sacramental studies have not been overwhelming.[1] When Thomas Aquinas and Bonaventure produced their first writings on the sacraments, their positions were also not immediately viewed as part of Catholic teaching. Many years after their lifetime, however, these two scholars became central to the Thomistic tradition and to the Franciscan tradition. Perhaps some of these sacramental writings will be honored in the same way.

In Chapter Four, I will present the beginnings of a theology of sacraments which is based on Section One in the *Catechism*'s discussion of sacraments. In my research, I have found the *Catechism* material on "Liturgy – The Work of the Holy Trinity" to be deeply religious and profoundly theological. I have no intention of saying that this sacramental presentation is the best possible presentation today. I simply want to share with my readers what I think is a remarkable theology of sacraments that meets many of the questions posed by Christians today.

Chapter four is divided into four parts.

I. Preliminary Observations Regarding the Background and Goals of Chapter Four

II. Which Understanding of the Trinity is at Work in Contemporary Literature's Presentation of Sacramental Theology?

III. A Sacramental Theology for Today – The Work of the Holy Trinity

IV. Conclusions

I. Preliminary Observations Regarding the Background and Goals of Chapter Four

In Chapter One, I began with the sacramental form that Edward Schillebeeckx presented in his 1960 book, *Christus, Sacrament van de Godsontmosting,* and which was translated into English as *Christ, the Sacrament of the Encounter with God* in 1963. Why did I start with Schillebeeckx? I began with him because his focus was on the humanity of Jesus as the foundational sacrament. Schillebeeckx's realization that the humanity of Jesus was a basic sacrament brought about a major change not only for sacramental theology but also for Christology. In both of these theological fields, major rethinking of sacramental theology has taken place. It was something absolutely new for a twentieth century Christian to believe that the humanity of Jesus Christ is the foundational sacrament of our encounter with God. This theological position radically changed the Christian way of understanding sacraments, since it went far beyond the long-lasting seven-sacrament position.

The next authors were Semmelroth and Rahner. Both men named the church as the foundational sacrament. This innovation also changed the entire structure of sacramental theology. The documents of Vatican II officially followed the new approach to sacramental theology, presenting the church as the foundational sacrament. The major change that the bishops made in the documents of Vatican II, however, was a new theology of the church, namely a new ecclesiology. The ecclesiological change had major repercussions on the way in which the seven sacraments can be understood. The conciliar bishops, however, did not focus directly on the seven sacraments and their relationship to the new ecclesiology. This relationship became a major discussion in post-conciliar theology.

The next official change in sacramental theology appeared in the *Catechism of the Catholic Church,* in which there are two different views of the sacraments. The first view, in my judgment, was groundbreaking since it presented the Trinity as the starting point of all sacramental life. The title of its main section bears this out: "Liturgy – work of the Holy Trinity." The second sacramental presentation—once again in my judgment—was basically a return to the pre-Vatican II, Neo-Scholastic theology of sacraments.

In this chapter, I want to focus on the Trinitarian approach to sacramental life. However, it is necessary to indicate the reasons why this Trinitiarian approach surpasses other sacramental approaches.

1. The Designation of the Humanity of Jesus as a Foundational Sacrament

Even though Schillebeeckx's book was published prior to Vatican II and even though the two books on sacraments by Semmelroth and Rahner had preceded his volume, I have chosen the volume by Schillebeeckx as my first entry because in his sacramental theology he taught that the humanity of Jesus was the primary sacrament. In this view, Jesus' humanity became the centralizing focus for all other aspects of

sacramental life. Schillebeeckx's approach became popular and helpful to many theologians and to many of the bishops at Vatican II.

Moving beyond the position of Schillebeeckx on the humanity of
Jesus, I would go so far as to designate the sacramental humanness of
Jesus as the original sacrament, the *Ursakrament*, or the fundamental
and originating sacrament. This designation was also a major step in
our contemporary rethinking of Christian sacramentality. This Christological interconnection entwines the Church as well as the seven
sacraments more closely to Jesus. This position emphasizes that each
of the seven sacraments as well as the church as a sacrament can be
understood only in and through Christology. In contemporary times,
the position that the humanity of Jesus is a fundamental sacrament
was the first major step that theologians took in their re-evaluation of
the sacraments.

2. The Designation of the Church as a Foundational Sacrament

A second step took place when contemporary theologians designated
the church itself as a foundation sacrament, the *Ursakrament*. In 1960,
as previously noted, Otto Semmelroth published a book in which the
church was the primary sacrament: *Vom Sinn der Sakramente*. In 1965,
the year in which Vatican II ended, Emily Schossberger translated
Semmelroth's book into English as *Church and Sacrament*. A number
of bishops at Vatican II were conversant in German, so Semmelroth's
volume was helpful to many of the conciliar bishops. Semmelroth was
very clear that the church had been instituted by Christ and he was
against a church that was portrayed as individualistic or collectivistic.
His book's major emphasis is on a correct understanding of the church.
For Semmelroth, the church consists of an institutional priesthood and
another part of the church we call the laity. Jesus established the church

as a sacrament in a two-fold way: the priestly aspect of the church as sacrament and the lay aspect of the church as sacrament. Moreover, Semmelroth explained that the church had a vertical dimension which can be called salvation. The whole church has been gifted by God with eternal salvation. A second dimension of the church is its depth, for Christ's command to the church was to bring faith to all people in the world. There is also a horizontal dimension of the church in which the church is socially active in the needs of today's world. The church is a sacrament in and through all three of these dimensions, for it manifests the forgiving love of God vertically, deeply and horizontally, and it does so in two different ways. In the church, the priest is one form of the ecclesial sacrament while the lay-person in the church is another form of the ecclesial sacrament.

Semmelroth's book on the church as a foundational sacrament is extremely helpful because his focus on the church and its multitude of dimensions offers a strong description of what the Church as sacrament means. His understanding of church was defensive and in many ways rather narrow, but he was dealing with some writers who were focused on the social action of the Church or on other ecclesial aspects. In particular he was challenging the views found in Emil Brunner's book, *Misunderstanding of the Church*.

The third volume that I previously mentioned was Karl Rahner's *Kirche und Sakrament*, which was published in 1961. In 1963, W. J. O'Hara published an English version entitled *The Church and the Sacraments*. We have seen that this volume had a major influence on the bishops at Vatican II since Rahner himself was a peritus at the council. In this volume, Rahner did not state that Jesus was a sacrament, use the term *Ursakrament*, or cite Semmelroth. However, in his essay, "Zur Theologie des Symbols," which he wrote in 1962, he does cite Semmelroth and in a footnote he even refers to the humanity of Jesus as a sacrament.

Rahner takes to task many Catholic theologians whose ecclesiology does not correspond to the historical developments of the Church that have been made in the twentieth century. One finds in his work an ecclesiology in conformity with the documents of Vatican II.[2] Although he entitles his lengthy first chapter as "The Church as the Church of the Sacraments," his opening section of this chapter is entitled, "The Church as the Fundamental Sacrament."[3] This means that the Church has many sacraments because the church itself is a fundamental sacrament. The church is the *Ursakrament.*

If a teacher is looking for excellent material on today's theology of sacrament, I would recommend Rahner's many writings on the sacraments. What he says about sacraments and what Schillebeeckx says about Jesus' humanness as the original sacrament are two important and complementary statements on the issue of the sacraments fifty years after Vatican II. A sacramental teacher today needs to have a solid background on the works of Schillebeeckx, Semmelroth, and Rahner. This is true, even though—as I am doing in this chapter—the teacher moves on to a totally new dimension of sacramentality, namely Trintarian sacramentality.

3. The Official Designation of the Church as a Foundational Sacrament

In the material just presented, only major theologians were cited. In section three, we move to more demanding level of authority, namely the documents of Vatican II. In Chapter One of this present volume, we focused on the citations in which the documents of Vatican II to describe the church as the basic sacrament. In Chapter Three, we examined the ways in which the conciliar documents took into account the history of the seven sacraments. Because the main focus in the Vatican II documents was on ecclesiology, one would not expect any developed and detailed consideration of the history of the seven sacraments. However, we found two issues that are of major importance today for a theology of sacraments.

- First of all, the single mention of *veluti sacramentum* cannot be used to interpret the bishops' use of church, which appears in many other passages of the Vatican II documents. Today, there are some authors who want to minimize the sacramentality of the church in the conciliar documents by their interpretation of *veluti*, which occurs only once and which in itself has several layers of meaning. This theological approach is invalid, since the overwhelming conciliar use of the phrase, the church is a sacrament, has no connection at all to the once-only-used adverbial restriction, veluti.

- Secondly, at the gathering of periti at University of Notre Dame and in the publication of their presentations and discussions, *Vatican II: An Interfaith Appraisal*, the scholars in attendance stated over and over that the bishops at Vatican II clearly wanted to say that the church was a sacrament. The affirmation of these scholars cannot be set aside. Theologians today who maintain that the conciliar bishops understood the church only as "veluti sacramentum" are placing themselves above the periti just mentioned. These nay-saying theologians were not periti at the council, and therefore do not have the depth of knowledge which the periti gathered at the university of Notre Dame exhibited.

For a sacramental teacher fifty years after Vatican II, the documents should be presented in a way which states clearly that the bishops understood the church as a sacrament, and that ecclesial sacramentality is fundamental to the conciliar change in ecclesiology. Secondly, the church as a sacrament is not simply one sacrament among many other sacraments. Rather, the church is a form which can be called an original sacrament, an *Ursakrament*. This means that the sacramentality of the church defines the meaning not only of the seven sacraments but also the meaning of sacramentals.

In the final pages of my examination of the documents of Vatican II in Chapter One, I mentioned that the position that the church as a sacrament would have little to no spiritual meaning if the bishops at Vatican II had not also used the phrase *Lumen Gentium*. In those final pages, I cited a book written in 1971, six year after Vatican II, by a peritus at the Council, Bonaventure Kloppenburg.

Kloppenburg stressed the title, *Lumen Gentium*. He explained how and why this title was given and how it was not simply a title that would honor John XXII. Rather, the title has a central focus for the Church, since *Lumen Gentium* gives us an inside look at the meaning of the incarnation. The human Jesus is the light whereby all women and men can see something of God. The presence of the Logos in Jesus is the reason why we can call Jesus *"Lumen."* When God sent the Logos into the humanity of Jesus, this incarnational presence of the Logos was to be a manifestation of God's love for us, and we are the *"Gentium."* The *"Lumen"* of Jesus is also the light that we Christians reflect. We are Christians only when we, as the moon, reflect the sunlight of Jesus.

There is a helpful history of this theological understanding of *Lumen Gentium*. In 1140, a major medieval theologian, Peter Lombard, completed his four volume book referred to as *The Sentences*. These volumes became the textbooks for all theological students from the early thirteenth century to the middle of the seventeenth century. As a major part of their training, theological students were required to teach courses in which they commented on major parts of these four volumes. If their lectures were not acceptable, they would not receive a doctoral degree.

In volume one of *The Sentences*, Peter Lombard focused on the one God and then on the Trinitarian God. As he focused on the Trinity, Peter Lombard raised the question about God's relationship to the created world.[4] For a Christian, there are two relationships: the relationship of the Logos to the humanity of Jesus, and the relationship of the Holy Spirit to many realities one finds in both the Old and New Testament.

Peter Lombard addressed the two relationships in the following way. First of all, God freely willed to send the Logos and the Spirit to human life. Lombard calls this sending *missio*. The sending is an important aspect of our relationship to God, since we creatures would have no assurance that God exists unless God in one way or another related to us first. We could guess that there is a God, and we might even try to believe that there is a God, but in both instances there is no "proof" that God exists.

A *missio*, however, would remain unnoticed unless God also provided a *manifestatio*. This was Peter Lombard's second position. The *manifestatio* of the Logos took place in the union of the divine nature with the human nature of Jesus. The human nature of Jesus is the visible manifestation of God. Jesus' human nature, however, is created, limited, and dependent. Consequently, his human nature manifests only some aspects of God. In his created humanity, there is no full manifestation of God. This does not mean that the manifestation is misleading; it simply means that in Jesus we have only a glimpse of the infinite beauty, wonder, and love of God. One could also speak of

Abraham, Moses, David and Solomon as a *missio* and *manifestatio*.[5] In Jesus, however, the Christian Church has believed that his manifestation of God is the greatest and that no other manifestation of God will take place until the end of the world.

Since the earliest centuries, Christian theologians have not been unanimous over the *manifestatio* of the Holy Spirit. For some, the manifestation of the Holy Spirit took place in the dove hovering above Jesus during his baptism. For others, the tongues of fire in the upper room shortly after the resurrection of Jesus were the manifestation of the Holy Spirit. There are several other examples that Christian theologians have suggested and Peter Lombard mentions a few of them. In fact, for many Christian theologians today, the Holy Spirit is free to use any created reality as the *manifestatio*. In other words, the Holy Spirit is not only sent by God, but he is manifesting his mission in hundreds of different ways.

Today, we use a different term for both the mission and manifestation, namely, the human nature of Jesus is the sacrament of the Logos (the manifestation), and the Logos was sent by God in order to reveal to us who God is (the mission). The sending of Jesus is the *missio* and the human nature of Jesus is the *manifestatio*. This is the basis of Christian belief. A mission without a manifestation was unthinkable to the theologians from the thirteenth to the seventeenth century. Peter Lombard thought in a medieval way, but his insight into mission and manifestation continues to have validity in one way or another even in the twenty-first century.

4. The Designation of Sacramental Life as the Work of the Trinity

The material in the *Catechism* on the Trinity and sacramental life was and still is a powerful insight (Section One). For me, this description substantiated a view that I had learned from my study of Augustine, Thomas Aquinas, Bonaventure and John Duns Scotus. This fundamental view can be described as follows: every major theologian's presentation of God has influenced and colored all the other aspects of his or her specific theology.

The title in the *Catechism* reads: "Liturgy – The Work of the Holy Trinity." The authors begin with the Trinity in order to understand sacramental theology. The Trinitarian God, therefore, shapes, colors and forms all other aspects of Christian theology including creation and incarnation, salvation, ecclesiology, and the seven sacraments. A class on sacraments which begins with a presentation on sacramental liturgy as the work of the Holy Trinity offers us a totally new understanding of Christian sacramentality.

Since the Trinitarian sacramentality is both new and powerful, Catholic teachers need to have a good grasp of where and how it originated. The text describing Trinitarian sacramentality is in the *Catechism of the Catholic Church*; therefore I want to explain how and why its presence in the *Catechism* is important.

5. The Presentation of the Seven Sacraments as Found in the *Catechism*

I have read and re-read Section Two of the *Catechism* many times. At first, I was puzzled by the way in which the material was developed. I did not find any substantial connection of the material in Section Two (§§1210-1690) with the material in Section One (§§1076-1209). As mentioned in previous chapters, I came to the conclusion that two different authors or two different groups of authors had written Section One and Section Two. I also compared the material with the pre-Vatican II presentation of the sacraments and found, for the most part, major similarities. I have already expressed my position with Section Two of the *Catechism*, so I will not include it in this present chapter.

Catechists today should be aware of this two-fold presentation of sacraments in the *Catechism* and their students should also be instructed on the presence of the two differing sacramental theologies in the *Catechism*.

6. There is a major caveat that remains even today. It is not fully developed, but it is central to the very meaning of sacrament.

In every divine mission and divine manifestation of God, there is a major issue that most theologians do not want to face. A sacrament is a manifestation of God in and through a created reality. In sacramental theology, we believe that God is present in some form or another in the humanity of Jesus, in the church, and in the individual sacraments.

I have just mentioned the mission and manifestation of God in the writings of Peter Lombard and in the sacraments there is a "manifestation" of God to some degree or another. There is also a "mission" of the Logos or Holy Spirit so that we will make God more present in our lives and hopefully in the lives of others. However, the manifestation of the Logos or of the Holy Spirit was not and is not a full manifestation of God. The basic reason for this limitation is the infinity of God.

In the Index of *Denzinger*, there is no listing for "infinite." When one looks through the many earliest creeds that are in *Denzinger*, none of them state: "we believe in an infinite God." For the early church, "we believe in an all-powerful God" was the more common phrase.[6] None of these creeds say "we believe in an infinite God," but almost all of these creeds say that "we believe in an all-powerful God." In *Denzinger*, the first time the word infinite appears is in a response from the Sacred Congregation for Indulgences in 1840 (§2751). A more important use of infinite appears in *Dei Filius* of Vatican I, (§3001), which was published in 1870. In the four-volume work, *Sacrae Theologiae Summa*, the first discussion on God's infinity appears in v. II, §§96-106, and the author, Joseph Dalmau, is focused on contemporary rationalists.

However, in the Middle Ages all the major theologians used the term infinite and John Duns Scotus became the most influential major scholar to write about the infinity of God. Since God is infinite, there is no possible manifestation of an infinite God to a finite human being. Our minds are unable to grasp anything infinite. This issue will be discussed more fully in a later section, but the relationship of an infinite God to sacramental theology is an intrinsic relationship. Sacramental theology today cannot be validated unless the issue of divine infinity becomes part of the conversation.

The manifestations of God to a human person, therefore, give us only a glimpse of God, a loving glimpse of a wonderful God that overwhelms us with its beauty and because of which we can say in all honesty, "I believe in God." Jesus' humanity, as the God-given *Lumen Gentium*, provides us with many wonderful glimpses of God. As a sacrament, the human nature of Jesus has manifested a glimpse of God to many, many people. When the women and men in the Catholic Church reflect something of this manifestation of God, then the sacramental Catholic Church is sacramentally exhibiting the blessings of God the Father, the love of Jesus, and the care and wisdom of the Holy Spirit.

The beauty and strength of the theology described above, at least as I see it, has the following wonderful components. First of all, it is a theology of sacraments that does not begin with the church, with priesthood, or with canon law. Rather, it begins with the Trinitarian God. Secondly, all sacraments are celebrated by the *Christus totus* and not simply by an individual Christian who is legally proficient, and who is legally acceptable. Thirdly, sacraments are celebrated by women and men who reflect the *Lumen* of Jesus, since no human person has any light at all. All of us constitute the mystery of the moon.

II. Which Understanding of the Trinity is at Work in Contemporary Literature's Presentation of Sacramental Theology?

In 2011, Cambridge University Press published a volume entitled *The Cambridge Companion to the Trinity*. The editor is Peter Phan.[7] The essays in this volume provide us with a wide range of Trinitarian theology, which leads us to ask: can sacramental theology and practice be renewed today if it is fundamentally experienced as the work of the Trinity? Which theology of Trinity should we use?

In his opening chapter, Phan notes that in spite of all the references to Father, Son, and Holy Spirit that one finds in the New Testament, "it does not mean that a full-fledged doctrine of the Trinity is already developed in the New Testament." He proceeds to inform us that "the road that leads from the New Testament's embryonic affirmations on the Trinity to contemporary Trinitarian theologies is a long, meandering, and tortuous one, at times disappearing and reappearing in the thicket of Christian doctrines."[8] The Trinitarian God is the heart of Christian doctrine and Christian life, but in the first century, a Trinitarian doctrine was not the pivotal foundation.[9] At other times, such as the post-Reformation period (1600 to 1900), the hierarchical church, not the Trinity, became the foundation of sacraments. Catholic sacraments were sacraments of the Catholic Church. Anglican and Protestant Churches did not have any valid sacraments.

We find a theology of Trinity disappearing and reappearing in the New Testament itself. Elaine Wainwright offers a brief overview of contemporary approaches by biblical scholars vis-à-vis the Trinity. She states that there is no one way to discover Trinitarian teaching in the New Testament.[10] There are several biblical scholars who would carefully admit that "there is no doctrine of the Trinity but there is material for the development of a doctrine."[11]

In the three Western Catholic traditions, Augustinian, Thomistic, and Franciscan, the respective theologies of the Trinity play a centralizing role. We have seen that one's theology of God is the basic influence on all other aspects of one's theology, which is true for Augustine, Thomas Aquinas, Bonaventure and Scotus. Based on the Trinitarian foundation, one moves to creation and to incarnation. Creation and incarnation, in the Catholic world, are intrinsically related. In the Augustinian and Thomistic tradition, God creates the universe and above all God creates human life. The incarnation of the Logos is not centrally connected to their theologies of creation. The incarnation of the Logos finds its place only after the sin of Adam and Eve. In the Franciscan tradition, however, the act of creation included God's sending of the Logos (*missio*) and the manifestation (*manifestatio*) of the Logos in the humanity of Jesus. The sending of the Logos into the humanity of Jesus is, in the Franciscan tradition, not based on the sin of Adam and Eve. Rather, the incarnation of the Logos was in God's original plan of creation. These differences influence the meaning of salvation. In Augustine and in Thomas, original sin plays a major role for their presentation of salvation. Let us examine the theology of Augustine on the union of Trinity, creation, incarnation, and salvation.

1. The Augustinian Understanding of Trinity

In Michel René Barnes's article, "Latin Trinitarian Theology," he analyzes in a careful way Augustine's movement from God's Trinitarian nature to creation and salvation.[12] One can find many changes in the Trinitarian theology of Augustine because he was searching for a correct way to understand the Trinity. Barnes, however, notes that there are three issues which remain foundational in Augustine's writings on the trinity:

a) First: Augustine's Teaching on God's Immaterial Nature

Barnes argues that this position in Augustine's theology was uniquely his. "What is distinctive to Augustine's theology, compared with the theologies of other late Nicenes, is the emphasis he places on divine immateriality to anchor the distinction between uncreated and created natures."[13] Intellectually, immateriality-materiality is the main hallmark of the division of uncreated nature and created nature. There is no in-between nature or "third nature."

b) Second: for Augustine, this doctrine of the common operations in the Trinity is also foundational.

Augustine carefully moves to a major conclusion vis-à-vis divine immateriality: "Augustine understands that the perfect immateriality of divine existence makes possible a degree of common operation that is otherwise impossible, and that to the degree that one removes a materialist way of thinking about the Trinity from ones theology then the perfectly common operations of the Trinity become a meaningful way of speaking about divine unity."[14] It is in Augustine's study of divine immateriality and its relation to common operation that he selects the similitude of memory, intelligence and will for his Trinitarian doctrine.

In Anne Hunt's volume, *Trinity: Nexus of the Mysteries of Christian Faith*, she notes that Augustine presents more than twenty triadic psychological analogies for exploration. He finally selected as the best analogy the interplay of intelligence, memory, and will-love.[15] She cites a major passage from Augustine:

> You know that in the Catholic faith it is the true and firm
> belief that the Father and the Son and the Holy Spirit are one
> God, while remaining a Trinity, because they are inseparably
> of the one and the same substance, or, if this is a better word,
> essence. … It remains for us, then, to believe that the Trinity
> is of one substance and that the essence is nothing else than
> the Trinity itself.[16]

In Augustine, however, establishing the substance or essence of God as totally separate from any and every created substance or essence was accomplished theologically by his insistence on divine immateriality. Only when this separation of the natural and the supernatural is clearly identified can one can ask about the inter-relational life of Father, Son, and Spirit.

c) Third: For Augustine there is the doctrine that theological language is meant to purify our thoughts about God as a necessary precondition to thinking about God as well as, for the greater end, seeing God.[17]

For human beings, Trinitarian language is meant to be salvational. The Word (Logos) is spoken to us to purify our thoughts and lead us to seeing God. Neither Barnes nor Hunt clearly express the issue of original sin, but this third issue can only make sense if we understand human nature to be sinful and therefore opposed to God. From many other statements of Augustine, we realize that original sin is a centerpiece of his view of human nature. After the sin of Adam and Eve, human beings had the power to sin (*posse peccare*). Through the incarnation, human beings were given the possibility of not sinning (*posse non peccare*). In heaven, human beings will have no power to sin (*non posse peccare*). In the theology of Augustine, therefore, the incarnation is salvational because human beings had already sinned. Consequently, the relationship of creation to incarnation came about because of the sin of Adam and Eve. Had they not sinned, the incarnation would not have

taken place.

This is a legitimate theological view and the doctrine of original sin has been a part of western theology particularly from Augustine onward. Sacramental actions are focused on removing human nature from sin to salvation. We see this in many theologies of baptism and reconciliation and anointing of the sick. The blessing of a marriage came to seen theologically as a removal of sexual deviation to sexual acceptance. Ordained ministers administered the sacraments so that sinners could be saved. In other words, an understanding of the Trinity, such as that of Augustine, colors the meaning of church and the meaning of the sacraments.

When we say that the liturgy is the work of the Holy Trinity and when we understand the Holy Trinity in an Augustinian way, then the focus of God's work is salvation from sin; this position affects our theological understanding of sacraments. It is a good effect, not a bad effect, but in the Augustinian view, salvation from our sinful state is almost omnipresent. In the sacraments, God is reaching out in love in order to give us the grace of salvation.

2. The Thomistic Understanding of Trinity

In the *Cambridge Companion to the Trinity*, Anselm Kyongsuk Min is the author of an article entitled "God as the Mystery of Sharing and Shared Love: Thomas Aquinas on the Trinity."[18] However, in 2005, Min had written a lengthy book, *Paths to the Triune God: An Encounter between Aquinas and Recent Theologies*.[19] It is in and through these two studies that we will consider the Trinitarian view of Thomas Aquinas and its relationship to sacramental liturgy as the work of the Holy Trinity.

Min, in his article on Thomas's view of the Trinity, states the focus of his work in the following way:

The most important systematic question of all Trinitarian

theology is perhaps the question concerning the origin of plurality or threeness in God, a being whose very essence is so uniquely "one" as to be "simple" in the sense of having no internal ontological composition in the way that finite entities do. How can there be three persons in the one God whose very essence is identical with his existence?[20]

There is no question that Thomas had studied the Trinitarian teaching of Augustine, and that he shares some of Augustinian structures as he reshapes his own teaching on the Trinity. In the above citation we see the phrase: internal ontological composition. Augustine had used the terms immateriality and common operation. These terms have some identity with the phrase that Thomas uses, namely internal ontological composition.

For Thomas' issue of distinction and plurality in God, Min presents many pages on the way Thomas develops relationality in God. He concludes this section of his essay as follows:

> There is no incompatibility, then, between person and relation. Because of the peculiarity of divine persons, "person" means relation not only by custom and stipulation but also by its own proper meaning. Only it means relation not by way of relation but by way of substance of *hypostasis*, that is, relation as subsisting in the divine nature (*Summa Theologiae*, 1, q. 20, a. 4).[21]

The Trinity in Thomas, then, is relational, and when we speak about sacramental liturgy as the work of the Holy Trinity, we need to perceive that the Trinitarian God in this liturgical work is eminently relational. In the *Catechism*, God the Father is portrayed again and again as blessing, and blessing is clearly a relational reality. In the *Catechism*, the chief words used to indicate Christ's work in the liturgy are: Christ gives us the Holy Spirit; Christ is present to us; it is Christ who baptized us; and he speaks to us in his gospel words. These are all relational phrases. In the section on the Holy Spirit in the liturgy, the relational words are abundant: the Holy Spirit teaches us; he arouses in us a response of faith; he makes Christ manifest; he recalls the mystery of Christ. Again, these are all relational terms and phrases. The Trinitarian God, in the theology of Thomas Aquinas, is a relational God.

3. The Franciscan Understanding of the Trinity

Before I begin the explanation of the Franciscan understanding of the Trinity, I have to confess that I am not impartial. I signed into the Franciscan seminary when I was only twelve years old and now I am eighty-three. For seventy-one years I have been "Franciscanized." However, in the sections above on Augustine and on Thomas, I hope I have presented honest descriptions of the relationality of God. Both theologies of the Trinity, in their respective ways, are able to form a theological basis for sacraments in which the primary aspect is: "liturgy, the work of the Holy Trinity." For both Augustine and Thomas, their understanding of God influenced and colored all other aspects of their theological work.

To grasp the understanding of Trinity in the Franciscan theological tradition, one must begin with St. Francis and St. Clare. Jean François Godet-Calogeras, in his essay, "Evangelical Radicalism in the Writings of Francis and Clare of Assisi," states in a very clear way the religious depth of their belief in God.

> For Francis and Clare, to follow Jesus is to imitate Jesus, that is, to become an image of Jesus, to become like him, perfect like God is perfect, nothing less.[22]

It was in their meditations on Jesus that both Francis and Clare came to an understanding of who God is. The God of Jesus is love, but especially unconditional love. Jesus was definitely the teacher who spoke about a compassionate and loving God. Alexander of Hales, one of the major early Franciscan theologians, expresses the goodness of

God as the origin of the Trinity. In his *Summa Theologica*, he asks a forthright question: why is there a three-fold numbering in God? His answer is deeply Franciscan. No necessity, he writes, not even internal necessity, requires God – Father, Word, and Spirit – to create. Creation is due to the goodness and wisdom of God, appropriated respectively to the Spirit and to the Word, and not merely due to the unnecessitated power of God appropriated to the Father.[23]

Two major issues are involved in a fundamental way in the Franciscan understanding of God. In the Trinitarian theology of Bonaventure, God is basically described as: *"bonum est sui diffusivum"* – "goodness is self-diffusive." This issue comes from his studies of some of the Eastern theologians and from Alexander of Hales. Bonaventure's Trinitarian theology is totally different from that of Augustine and Thomas Aquinas. Bonaventure's theology corresponds in a profound way with the diffusive goodness of the Trinity as presented in the First Section of the *Catechism,* entitled "Liturgy – The Work of the Holy Trinity."

Whether Augustinian, Thomistic, or Franciscan, the following diagram is meant to show the interrelationship of all theological aspects within one's theology of God. It is my view that we must continually return to the theology of God whenever we are considering other aspects, such as baptism or anointing of the sick, preaching or ministry, spirituality and prayer. One's theological and spiritual view of God is the lens through which one tries to see everything else. The phrase, "sacramental liturgy – the work of the Holy Trinity" places God at the very beginning of one's theology of sacrament. For sacramental theology, one does not start with church, nor does one allow canon law to dominate sacramental explanation. Rather, one's theology of the Trinitarian God is the point of departure of all created life. With this in mind, let us consider the following diagram.

Seven Sacraments

The Church Foundational Sacrament

Jesus in His Human Nature *(Ursakrament)* is the Sacrament of God

Creation — Incarnation

The Holy Trinity **Creator of Heaven and Earth**

This diagram can be read from top down, in which one moves from the seven sacraments to the church as a sacrament. The seven sacraments find their meaning in the more foundational sacrament, the church itself. The theology of church as a foundational sacrament is a major position in the documents of Vatican II, but the church as a foundational sacrament finds its meaning in Jesus, the *Lumen Gentium*. The bishops at Vatican II did not present Jesus as a basic sacrament, but in current theology there are many important authors for whom the human nature of Jesus is the most basic sacrament, the *Ursakrament*, since in the human life of Jesus we discover a reflection of the Trinitarian God and, as the *Catechism* states, the sacramental liturgy is the "work of the Holy Trinity." In this diagram, we can move from the seven sacraments to the Trinity.

If we move from the bottom to the top, there is something deeply characteristic of every theology that has become a tradition within a given Christian community. This special aspect is that one's theology of God shapes, forms, infuses and gives meaning to everything else. The "everything else" in the diagram includes creation-incarnation, Jesus in his human nature, the church and the seven sacraments. One's theology of God also affects the presence of the Holy Spirit in the lives of all men and women.

The reason that I am urging this is the following: *let your theology of the Trinitarian God influence all other aspects of theology as deeply as you can.*

The Trinity within the Franciscan tradition cannot be fully understood unless one also considers a major aspect of the theology of God, namely that God is infinite. In the Middle Ages, no theologian studied the infinity of God more than John Duns Scotus. In 1954, Allan B. Wolter delivered an address to the American Catholic Philosophical Association entitled "Duns Scotus and the Existence and Nature of God."[24] In his presentation, Wolter explains that Scotus came to the conclusion that God's infinity is not an attribute of God; rather, the very essence of God is infinite. This means that there is only one infinite God and infinity is an integral aspect of the one God. If one attempts to talk about God and does not include infinity, one is not talking about God. This was clearly the emphasis which Scotus developed.

This view has major ramifications. For our purposes, it means that no human being can fully understand the infinite God. In the *Catechism*, the opening pages speak about God and the ways in which many human beings have sought knowledge of God. "Our knowledge of God is limited, our language about him is equally so" (§40). However, later in the *Catechism* one reads: "God has revealed himself fully by sending his own Son, in whom he has established his covenant forever" (§73). If Scotus were alive today, he would ask how an infinite God can "reveal himself *fully?*"

If God is infinite, then no human person, no religious group, no philosophical trend can ever say that they have full knowledge of God. Given the inter-religious discussions which have developed since Vatican II, can we Catholics claim that "our God" is the one and only God? If we claim this, are we limiting an infinite God? I am not making any judgments, but if God is infinite, then any form of limiting God becomes questionable.

III. A Sacramental Theology for Today – The Work of the Holy Trinity

Imagine that you are in a classroom with a group of teenagers, and you are teaching them sacramental theology when questions arise. Why should I be confirmed? Why do I have to be married in the church? Why do I have to receive the Eucharist? Why do I have to go to confession? These are all legitimate questions and generally teachers give answers that are based on Church regulations.

However, if our starting point is God's action on us, then the entire framework of the discussion is changed. One moves to a more foundational sacramental reality, namely "The Liturgy – the Work of the Holy Trinity." In this format all sacraments are primarily the work of God. For example, theologians say today that the humanity of Jesus is the foundational sacrament. However, the relationship between the humanity of Jesus and God the Father is blessing, for God has blessed us by sending Jesus, and God has blessed the humanness of Jesus so that we can see God in a clearer way. In this framework, our answers to the student's questions are not citations from Church law or from a theology of church. Rather, we answer the student's question by stating that in all of the sacraments mentioned, it is primarily God who is blessing us. We need the sacraments of confirmation, marriage, Eucharist, and reconciliation because in these sacraments God is blessing each one of us. God's blessing is the most fundamental aspect of each and every sacrament. The teacher, then, can respond to the student's question by saying, "Don't you want God to bless you? God blesses us you in confirmation. God blesses a new couple in the sacrament of marriage. God blesses each student when he or she receives communion. God blesses each student in the sacrament of reconciliation." In all of these instances, the action of the priest or bishop is secondary. Even the actions of the students are secondary. God wants to bless us and God wants to do this in a special way in and through the sacraments.

Blessings are gifts. The Logos did not have to become flesh in the humanity of Jesus, but God gifted us with the Word made flesh. Jesus as the foundational sacrament fulfills in a special way what sacraments are about, namely that God the Father is blessing us in and through the sacraments. Every sacrament is a sacrament *of* something and a sacrament *to* someone. The human Jesus is a sacrament *of* God's love, blessing, and care, and the human Jesus is a sacrament *to* everyone who reads about him and believes in him.

One might say that the church is a sacrament. Again we ask *of* what and *for* whom. As a sacrament, the church is a reflection *of* Jesus, the *Lumen Gentium* and the church is a sacrament *for* all those who can see this reflection of the *Lumen Gentium*. Kloppenburg expresses this situation in a very direct way:

> If the church is absolutized, separated from Christ, considered only in its structures, viewed only in its history, and studied only under its visible, human, and phenomenologi-

cal aspects, it ceases to be a "mystery" and becomes simply one of countless other religious societies or organizations. It does not then deserve our special attention and total dedication. Only because it is a "mystery" can it arouse our love.[25]

The church is mystery but in a special way. The church is the mystery of the moon and Jesus is the mystery of *Lumen Gentium*. In the Church, we experience this mystery of the moon and the mystery of Jesus who is the *Lumen Gentium* when we experience what the Trinity is doing in each and all of our sacramental liturgies. What is the Trinity doing at confirmation, at Eucharist, at a marriage, at an ordination, at reconciliation, and at an anointing of the sick? The answer to these questions is overwhelmingly similar. The *Catechism* provides the answers.

- God the Father is blessing and blessing and blessing.

- Jesus is making the grace of God efficaciously present. He is making present the paschal mystery for all who are celebrating a sacrament. In the celebration of every sacrament Jesus is the true minister. Basically, it is Jesus who baptizes, Jesus who confirms, Jesus who forgives sin, etc.

- The Holy Spirit is bringing the gift of faith to those who are present. The Holy Spirit is transforming those who are present into the mystery of Christ. The Holy Spirit is uniting those who are present to the community called church. He is bringing spiritual understanding to all who share in the celebration of a sacrament. The Spirit makes present the mystery of Christ to those who are celebrating the sacrament.[26]

If the basis for sacramental theology is the work of the Holy Trinity, then theologians need to readdress the Trinitarian theology so that the theology of Trinity and the theology of sacraments are mutually interrelated. This focus on the Triune God is the first and foremost characteristic of a sacramental theology for today.

There is a second major focus in a sacramental theology for today. In the same chapter of the *Catechism* that states that sacramental liturgy is the work of the Holy Trinity, there is another key issue which enriches the very roots of a contemporary theology of sacraments. Two sentences from the *Catechism* capture this important aspect of sacramental theology.

> "Liturgy is an action of the whole Christ, *Christus totus*" (§1136).

> "It is the whole community, the Body of Christ united with its Head, that celebrates" (§1140).

These references from the *Catechism* help us to understand that the church is a foundational sacrament and that the humanity of Jesus is the *Ursakrament*. We see this in the wording which is used in the *Catechism*, namely "the whole Christ, *Christus totus*." In the Vatican documents, the bishops stated that the church is a sacrament, but the church is sacramental only because of *Christus totus*. It is in the church's union with *Christus totus* that the church can also be seen as a sacrament. Moreover, the *Christus totus* is sacramental because the *Christus totus* is the work of the Holy Trinity. The whole community celebrates each sacrament. It is not simply the priest who celebrates. The more communal the liturgy is, the more Christians will realize who is celebrating a sacrament.

There is a third aspect of sacramentality embedded in the work of the Holy Trinity and in the *totus Christus*. The most important document of Vatican II is entitled *Lumen Gentium*. Jesus is the light of the world. The church is church when Christians reflect the light of the world, Jesus. Jesus in his humanity reflects the Triune God and thereby his humanity is also a sacrament. The church is a sacrament when it reflects Jesus, but it can only do so if the church, in all its leadership, liturgy, and Christian living, is theologically understood as the mystery of the moon. No leadership, no liturgy and no Christian have any sacramental meaning if these realities are not reflecting Jesus. Just as the moon has no light of its own, the church has no light of its own. The church is a beautiful moon when it reflects Jesus and Jesus, who is the light of the world, reflects the Triune God. There is something sacramental about the phrase *Lumen Gentium*.

Whenever one speaks of a sacrament, two major questions arise: "sacrament of what" and "sacrament for whom?" The phrase *Jesus as Lumen Gentium* is basically focused on his human nature, for his human nature is a reflection of God (sacrament of what?). And since Jesus in his human nature is the sun, we can also say that the church is the moon. But the moon has no light of its own, the only light the moon has is the reflected light of the sun. Thus the second question, "To whom is Jesus a light?" can be answered when the Light of Jesus is reflected in the women and men of the church. Jesus is the light which is a reflection *of* God and a reflection *to* those in the church.

Let me repeat what I have written previously:

> In many ways, this approach [of the *Catechism*] to sacramental theology may be the most theologically helpful change for today's Christian life. I say this since the best Christian theological system has been written when one's theology of God shapes the ways through which all other theological positions are explained. A sacramental theology cannot begin simply with an explanation of the seven sacraments, nor can it begin simply with the church as the foundational sacrament, the *Ursakrament*. In a much more subtle way, sacramental theology does not even begin with the humanity of Jesus. In a most profound way, sacramental theology begins with the sacraments as the work of the Holy Trinity. God, the Holy Trinity, is the foundation on which all other parts of theology are formed and developed.

When we analyzed the statement that sacramental liturgy is the work of the Holy Trinity, we saw that in the section entitled "The Father – Source and Goal of the Liturgy," the word blessing was used again and again. God the Father blessed us in an overwhelming way. When we are teaching a course on the sacraments and are focusing on baptism, the important aspect of baptism is that "God is blessing" both the person to be baptized and the community in which the baptized will live.

When we ask what Christ's work in baptism is all about, the answer is: Jesus is giving us grace; Jesus is making the mystery of God present; Jesus is sending the baptized to proclaim the good news; Jesus entrusts the baptized with the power of the Holy Spirit.

When we ask what the Holy Spirit's work is all about, we have five pages in the *Catechism* from which we can select phrases. The Holy Spirit is teaching us, he arouses in us a deep faith, he prepares us to meet God, and he makes the mystery of Christ present within us. The list goes on.

The point that this is making can be expressed as follows:

- What is baptism? The first and most important answer is: what is the Trinity doing? In baptism, the Trinity is blessing the baptized and the family of the baptized.
- What is confirmation? What is the Trinity doing? In confirmation, the Trinity is confirming the one who is being confirmed and the faith of the women and men in the church who are close to one who is confirmed is also being strengthened by God.

The same kind of answers can be given in the other sacraments.

- What is Eucharist? What is the Trinity doing?
- What is reconciliation? What is the Trinity doing?

- What is marriage? What is the Trinity doing?
- What is ordination? What is the Trinity doing?
- What is anointing of the sick? What is the Trinity doing?

In other words, we do not start by asking: who is the minister? Who is able to receive the sacrament? What is the verbal form of the sacrament? What is the material element in the sacrament? What is the effect of the sacrament?

Rather, with each sacrament we ask first and foremost what the Trinitarian God is doing in each of the sacraments. This is a totally different starting point for teaching sacramental theology. It gives us a new view of sacraments, since the main thing about the seven sacraments is not what we do, nor is it what the church does or what an ordained priest does. These are all secondary and tertiary issues. The primary focus for understanding the seven sacraments is to perceive what God is doing in baptism, in confirmation, in Eucharist, etc. In teaching sacraments, we begin with what God is doing and only later, in a secondary way, do we consider what the church is doing and what an individual is doing. In this procedure, we have moved into a sacramental theology which can be called a "God-Centered Sacramental Theology."

However, we need to deepen this God-Centered Sacramental Theology; therefore the next step is to present the church as sacrament, which includes the issue of Jesus as *Lumen Gentium*. Of myself as a Christian, I have no light, and even though I might be baptized, confirmed, etc., I still have no light. However, if as a member of the church I try to reflect Jesus, the *Lumen Gentium*, then I am letting Jesus, the Light of the world, into my life.

At this juncture, the two first chapters of *Lumen Gentium* are crucial, because chapter one spells out the meaning and depth of Jesus, the *Lumen Gentium*, and chapter two's theme is the people of God who are invited to reflect the Light of Jesus. In chapter two, the conciliar bishops selected the title "People of God" so as to eliminate any hierarchical dimension. In §§ 10 and 11, the bishops included references to the hierarchical priesthood, but these references are brief. Many conservative bishops wanted chapter two to focus on the hierarchy, but this was not accepted. It seems that this was done to appease the conservative bishops. It is in chapter three of *Lumen Gentium* that the bishops center on ordained ministry, and ordained ministry makes sense only on the basis of chapter one, Jesus the *Lumen Gentium*, and on the basis of chapter two, which deals with all Christians in an equal way as the people of God.

In chapter two, the bishops refer to all the sacraments, but not in a way that we can call "Sacramental Liturgy - the Work of the Holy Trinity." Nor is there any mention of the *Christus totus*. Fifty years after Vatican II, we can understand the sacramental liturgy to be the work of the Holy Trinity, and we can speak about the *Christus totus* and about the opening statement in *Lumen Gentium* that describes Jesus as the "light of the nations." We can speak about the ways in which all Christians are similar to the moon which has no light of its own. Christians have no light except the light from Jesus, the *Lumen gentium*.

The above issues might take two or three weeks of a course on sacraments since it does require a detailed study of the first two chapter of *Lumen Gentium*, as well as a detailed study of the *Catechism* (§§1066-1209) and, as a suggestion, a study on a section from Kloppenburg's book, *The Ecclesiology of Vatican II* (pp. 12-39).

It is evident that this format for a course on the sacraments does not start with these words: "Christ instituted the sacraments of the new law. There are seven: Baptism, Confirmation, the Eucharist, Penance, the Anointing of the Sick, Holy Orders and Matrimony" (*Catechism*, §1210). Instead, the three keys to this format are:

- Sacramental Liturgy – the Work of the Holy Trinity
- It is the whole community—*Christus totus*, the body of Christ, united to Jesus the head—that celebrates
- Jesus is the *Lumen Gentium*; we are like the moon which has no light but whose beauty and meaning comes when we reflect the sun and our Sun is Jesus.

This sacramental approach is a contemporary theology of the Christian sacraments in which the Holy Trinity is the starting point. This contemporary effort includes many issues which have already been explained in the earlier chapters. The theology of sacraments, beginning with Jesus as the foundational sacrament, is a solid and strong presentation, and many contemporary theologians have explained the sacraments in and through the foundational sacrament, namely the humanity of Jesus. Likewise, the theology of sacraments, beginning with the church as the foundational sacrament, is another powerful way to theologize on the sacramental life of the Church today. This form of sacramental theology is found in the documents of Vatican II and in the writings of many contemporary scholars. Since this form of sacramental theology was incorporated, in some degree, into the documents of Vatican II, this form of sacramental explanation has gained a certain prestige.

Because there are five different approaches to a theology of sacraments today, it is important to keep in mind that each of the five ways has the acceptance by Church leadership and has a strong following among contemporary theologians. My selection of a sacramental theology based on the work of the Holy Trinity is also validated by Church leadership and is one of the major forms of contemporary sacramental theology. The fact that I prefer this form should not be seen as a belittling of the other four forms of contemporary sacramental theology in the Catholic Church.

The unfolding of this theology of sacraments is a step-by-step process that involves six successive stages.

STAGE	STEP
Stage one	The Holy Trinity – the foundation of creation and sacraments
Stage two	The interrelationship of creation and incarnation
Stage three	The humanity of Jesus as the foundational sacrament
Stage four	The people of God are like the moon. Only when they reflect the sun, Jesus, can they be the people of God. Only in this sense is the church a sacrament of Jesus and of the Trinitarian God.
Stage five	The seven sacraments
Stage six	The sacramentality of all creation

It is precisely the presence and the work of the Trinity in a sacramental celebration through which I see the true beginning of what a sacrament is all about. The foundation of sacramental life and theology is the Holy Trinity; everything else draws its existence and meaning from the position: Sacramental Liturgy – The Work of the Holy Trinity.

As an example, let us consider the meaning of the phrase, "Sacramental liturgy is the work of the Holy Trinity," apropos to the sacrament of reconciliation.

- In the celebration of reconciliation, God the Father is blessing, blessing, and blessing. The sinner confesses his or her sins and the response of God the Father is blessing. The sinful man or woman says "I have sinned" and God the Father says "I bless you."

- In the celebration of the sacraments of reconciliation, Jesus is the true minister. The sinful man or woman says "I have sinned," and Jesus the minister of the sacrament makes the "grace of God efficaciously present." He makes present "the paschal mystery" for all who are confessing their sins.

- In the celebration of the sacrament of reconciliation, the Holy Spirit brings to the sinner the gift of faith. The Holy Spirit transforms the sinner into the mystery of Christ. The Holy Spirit unites the sinner to the community called church, and he brings spiritual understanding to all who share in the celebration of the penitential sacrament. The Spirit makes present the mystery of Christ in each and every celebration of God's grace of reconciliation.

When I stand back and meditate on what the Father, Son, and Spirit are actually doing in a given sacrament, my mind and my heart open up to the unbelievable depth of sacramental life. The Trinitarian approach to the sacraments moves us beyond human and natural activities, for the work in the sacramental liturgies is first and foremost the work of the Holy Trinity. In this approach to sacramental life, one can deeply experience and respond to the blessing and blessing and blessing of the Father. One can also deeply respond to Jesus making God present to oneself, to Jesus making the Paschal Mystery present to oneself, to Jesus making himself the one and true sacramental minister, present to oneself. One can also deeply respond to the Holy Spirit, who is making the Paschal Mystery present and who is bringing the response of faith to all who share in the sacrament. The Holy Spirit transforms those who are present at the reconciling mystery, because the Spirit unites them more closely to the community called church and the Spirit gives them a deeper understanding of God's forgiving love.

In the theologies of the Catholic Church, the interrelationship of creation and incarnation has been presented in two differing ways. Creation and incarnation have been seen as two distinct actions of God. In the Augustinian and Thomistic theological traditions, God first created the world in all its stages, and in the book of Genesis the creation of human life is presented as God's final step in his creative action.

> God looked at everything he had made, and he found it very good. Evening came, and morning followed – the sixth day. Thus the heavens and earth and all their array were completed. Since on the seventh day God was finished with the work he had been doing, he rested on the seventh day from all the work he had undertaken (Gen. 1:31-2:2).

When Adam and Eve sinned, God sent them from the Garden of Eden but God also promised that human life would eventually be saved. There seems to be a faint indication that in the future, a savior would be born. From the biblical passages, Jesus came as the savior of the world. If Adam and Eve had not sinned, there would have been no need for such a savior.

In this approach, God's initial action of creation did not include the incarnation of the Logos in the human nature of Jesus. Rather, God sent his son as a savior of sinful people. Creation and Incarnation are two distinct acts of God.

In the Franciscan theological tradition, the primary action of God included the primary action of incarnation. God's actual creation also included the incarnation of Jesus. An understanding of creation cannot be avoided. It is a major part of the Christian belief that the world that surrounds us spatially and temporally has been created by God. Creation is a matter of belief; it is not an issue of intellectual rationalization. Consequently, contemporary scientists cannot be expected, in all their analyses of the universe, to come to the conclusion that God exists. Scientists today present us with a new way of looking at the microcosmic world, the quantum world. Scientists today also present us with a new way of looking at the macrocosmic world, a world that is multi-billions of years old. In the contemporary understanding of the microcosmic universe and the macrocosmic universe, scientists have not yet discovered an over-arching plan. Christian believers, Islamic believers, and Jewish believers all maintain that there is an over-arching plan for the universe, which they often refer to as salvation history. Once again, however, the Christian, Islamic, and Jewish men and women *believe* in the reality of salvation history. Salvation history is a matter of faith, not of logical reasoning.

The inclusive position, creation–incarnation, raises questions about salvation, since sin is clearly a matter of reality. In the Franciscan tradition, the second person of the blessed Trinity, the Logos, became flesh not because of the need of salvation, but rather the Logos became flesh in order to reveal the depth and breadth of divine salvation. Jesus' entire life, death, and resurrection were revelatory of who and what God is. God is a saving God because God is a loving and compassionate God.

The Franciscan theologian, Luc Mathieu, in his essay "Était-il nécessaire que le Christ mourût sur la croix?" carefully explains this inter-relationship of creation and incarnation:

> God's pardon of sin is an act of pure gratuity and pure benevolence which is intrinsic to the act of creation… There is no other necessity than the divine free will, God's gratuitous love, and God's omnipotence.[27]

> Was it necessary that humanity be restored and that Christ had to suffer? It is fitting that we never forget that the divine act of creation is gratuitous, just as all actions of God ad extra.[28]

The Franciscan theologian, Johannes Freyer, mentions that the

Franciscan theologians of the thirteenth century developed a unique soteriology. Franciscan soteriology is based on the Trinitarian God who is *bonum sui diffusivum* (Bonaventure) and based on the infinite free and loving will of God (Scotus).[29]

A theology of God does not mean that a human being has a thorough knowledge of God, nor does it mean that a human being has a thorough understanding of the central essence of God. In the Franciscan theological tradition of God, the infinity of God means that no human being will ever attain a full knowledge of who God truly is. In Scotus' teaching on the infinite God, especially in his final writings on this issue, one cannot speak of God unless one also acknowledges that God is infinite. For Scotus, Christians do not simply believe in God, they believe strongly in only one God. Scotus carries the theme of belief in one God even further, for Christians believe in one God who is infinite. Infinity is not a description of God that is added to the "existence of God." Rather, for Scotus the only actual God we believe in is a God who is both one and infinite. Augustine and Thomas clearly believed in one God, but for both theologians, the infinity of God was a quality that needs to be established on the basis that God exists. Only if we can believe that God exists can we then speak about the infinity of God. Scotus states that this basis is inadequate; the basis for a belief in God is both the oneness of God and the infinity of God.[30]

The relationship of creation and salvation certainly raises a major problem. Can this difficulty be resolved or is it simply untenable? In human life, we are faced with many positive-negative situations and issues. Whenever a negative situation or issue arises, human beings often examine the negativity in a detailed way. Is the negative situation or issue unexpected? Can the negative situation or issue be resolved? An author recently wrote a book entitled *Why Do Bad Things*

Happen to Good People? At the end of the book, the author states clearly that no fulfilling answer to the question can be given.

For someone who believes in God, there may be another answer. Namely, the presence and power of God who is good far surpasses the presence and power of any evil situation, for God's presence and power is infinite. At first, this answer appears unsatisfactory, but the answer is telling us to stop analyzing the evil situation and turn our attention to the goodness of God. The focus on God does not take away the evil, but it puts the evil into a different framework, a framework of goodness.

Human life is a mixture of good and bad, virtue and vice, limitation and expansion. Regardless of whether one believes in God or not, the world we live in cannot be seen as a totally good world. Our world is a limited world and disruption is a part of a limited world. Scientists examine destructive cosmic situations and constructive cosmic situations. The human body develops from a deeply dependent body of an infant, to the life-filled body of a teenager, to a basically mature body of an adult, down to a body which is beginning to show weakness as old age takes over. At every moment in this passage, there are strengths and weaknesses. Salvation does not mean that the weaknesses are eliminated from human life. Salvation focuses on the positive forces, not on the negative ones.

The documents of Vatican II were deliberately written in a way which would allow the Roman Catholic Church today to be more open to the contemporary world. *Lumen Gentium* opened the Church to a closer union to Jesus, the Light of the World (chapter one) and to the people of God (chapter two). The dogmatic constitution on divine revelation, *Dei Verbum*, carefully opened the Church to contemporary biblical hermeneutics. The Constitution on the Liturgy, *Sacrosanctum*

Concilium, opened the liturgy to the multi-cultural world. The decree on the lay person in the church, *Apostolicam Actuositatem*, opened the ministry of the church to lay women and men. The decree on ecumenism, *Unitatis Redintegratio*, opened the Church to dialogue and cooperation with Anglican, Protestant, and Free Christian Churches. The decree on relations with other religions, *Nostra Aetate*, opened the Church to cooperation with non-Christian religions.

In all of these documents, one can see an effort by the conciliar bishops to move the Church into the contemporary world. These different openings of the Church involve change, and in the fifty years after Vatican II the Roman Catholic Church has changed in all of the above areas.

IV. Conclusions

There are three major conclusions which emerge from the material expressed in this chapter:

1. In the past sixty years, there has been a theological rethinking of sacrament in the Catholic Church, and this rethinking of sacrament has been a blessing for the Catholic Community.

In part one, we considered the five major theologies on sacramentality:

a) That Jesus in his human nature is the foundational sacrament (Schillebeeckx)

b) That the church is a sacrament (Semmelroth and Rahner)

c) That the church is officially called a sacrament (documents of Vatican II)

d) That sacramentality is primarily the work of the Holy Trinity (*Catechism*)

e) That the seven sacraments were instituted by Jesus Christ (*Cat-*

echism)

This diversity of theological thought on the meaning of sacrament has had strong effects on the celebration of the liturgy and in the catechesis on sacramental life in the church. The fact that there are different views should not be considered as a time of confusion; rather, it demonstrates that Catholic leaders and scholars are rethinking an important part of Catholic life. We have already seen that the effects of this re-thinking have changed the liturgical celebration of each sacrament: more and more lay people are now involved in sacramental celebrations. Moreover, the renewed rites are, for the most part, more easily understood by the community at large.

There are some people in the church who want to retain the liturgical forms which were used prior to Vatican II. Even some of the Vatican Curia wanted to retain the former ways of celebrating the sacraments. As a consequence, there has been a tension in church leadership vis-à-vis sacramental celebrations.

2. Theological professors and catechists need to keep in mind that there are several forms of sacramental theology today. Those whom they teach should be given at least an overview of the various forms of sacramental theology.

The history of each of the sacraments was a major, though often unspoken, reason for the new approach to the sacraments. Teachers should be better informed of this history of the sacraments and also informed of the connection this history has with a "theology of sacraments."

Since there are three western theological traditions, these traditions should also be a part of the background for classes on the sacraments. In each tradition, the theology of God influences all other aspects of one's theology. It is important to understand the differences amongst the three differing theologies of the Trinity that can be found in the three traditions. Both the teacher and the students should understand the deep connection between one's theology of a Trinitarian God and all other aspects of a theology. This interconnection is the basis of why there are three differing Western Catholic traditions.

3. In this chapter, I have selected one approach to a theology of sacraments based on three issues: (a) sacramental liturgy is the work of the Holy Trinity; (b) the Christus totus celebrates each sacrament; (c) the profound meaning behind the phrase Lumen Gentium.

The basic reasons why I selected this form of sacramental theology are three-fold: first, it begins with God: "Sacramental Liturgy – The Work of the Holy Trinity." Secondly, in its description in the *Catechism* the question of who celebrates is given an answer: it is "The whole community, the Body of Christ united with the Head that celebrates." Thirdly, the title of the main document at Vatican II is *Lumen Gentium*, and the ecclesiology behind this title is extremely attractive: Jesus alone is the light of the world; the church has no light of its own so it resembles the moon. When the Church, in its sacramental dimensions, reflects the light of Jesus, it is church; when it reflects its own light it is not church.

A sacramental theology that begins in this way has not yet been fully developed. Much more theological discussion needs to be made on the sacramental theology, but its beginnings have been stated and hopefully in the future, this format for sacramental theology continues to grow.

Endnotes

1. See for example, William Bausch, *A New Look at the Sacraments*, (Mystic, CT: Twenty-Third Publications, 1983); Bernard Cooke, *Ministry to Word and Sacrament* (Fortress Press, 1976); Regis Duffy, *Real*

Presence (San Francisco: Harper& Row, 1982); Louis-Marie Chauvet, *Symbole et Sacrement: Un relecture sacramentelle d l'existence chrétienne* (Paris: Les Éditions du cerf, 1987). Many other authors could also be cited.

2. In 1965 to 1967, Karl Rahner was one of my professors at the University in Munich, at which I earned my doctorate. He has had a great deal of influence on me, since in his many lectures he was explaining what had been going on at Vatican II, not only publicly but in small conversations. I am deeply indebted to him.

3. Rahner, op. cit., 11.

4. Peter Lombard, *Libri IV Sententiarum*, (Grottaferrata-Rome: Collegium S. Bonaventurae ad Claras Aquas, 1971), Liber I, Dist. 14.to Dist. 18,

5. In today's inter-religious dialogues, there is much room for several *missiones* and *manifestationes* of God. Since God is infinite, no one religion can claim a "full knowledge" of God. These issues are discussed in *Science and Religion* (Eugene, OR: Wipf and Stock, 2013).

6. See *Denzinger*, §§17-42 for the *Symbola Fidei*, or early creeds. None of these creeds say: we believe in an infinite God, but they almost all say we believe in an all-powerful God. In *Denzinger*, the first time the word infinite appears in an official document is in a response from the Sacred Congregation for Indulgences, 1840, §2751. A more important use of infinite appears in *Dei Filius* of Vatican 1, §3001, which was promulgated in 1870. In *Sacrae Theologiae Summa*, the first discussion on God's infinity appears in v. II, §§96-106, and the author, Joseph Dalmau, is focused on contemporary rationalists. However, in the Middle Ages, all the major theologians used the term infinite in an abundant way, and John Duns Scotus became the major scholar to write about the infinity of God.

7. See *The Cambridge Companion to the Trinity*, ed. Peter Phan (New York: Cambridge University Press, 2011). This book will be referred to as CCT.

8. Phan, "Development of the Doctrine of the Trinity," CCT, 3-4.

9. See CCT. 16-24. In these pages, Phan explains three interrelated questions which have engendered the most difficulties for Trinitarian doctrine: first, is it possible to speak of the immanent, or transcendent, or ontological Trinity, that is, the eternal relations among Father, Son, and Spirit at all? Secondly, if the immanent Trinity is possible and even necessary, is the so-called psychological model that uses the human mind, namely Augustine's *mens* or *memoria*, with its twofold operation of knowing and loving (*intellegentia* and *amor*) as an analogy of the immanent Trinity, still valid and useful? Thirdly, how are the economic Trinity and the immanent Trinity interrelated to each other?

10. Elaine Wainwright, "Like a finger pointing to the moon: exploring the Trinity in/and the New Testament," CCT, 33-48.

11. See Arthur Wainwright, *The Trinity in the New Testament* (London: SPCK, 1962), 237-267, cited in Elaine Wainwright's article, 44.

12. Michel René Barnes, "Latin trinitarian theology," *CCT*, 70-84. For his section on Augustine see 78-82.

13. Ibid., 79.

14. Ibid., 79-80.

15. See Anne Hunt, *Trinity: Nexus of the Mysteries of Christian Faith*, 19-20.

16. See *Saint Augustine, Bishop of Hippo, Letters*, v. 2 (83-130), Eng. trans. by Wilfred Parsons, in *Fathers of the Church*, v. 18 (Washington, D.C.: Catholic University of America Press, 1953), 311.

17. Barnes, op. cit., 79, but see also 81-82.

18. See Anselm Kyongsuk Min, "God as the mystery of sharing and shared love: Thomas Aquinas on the Trinity," *CCT*, 87-107. Henceforth, this article will be referred to as *Min I*.

19. Anselm Kyongsuk Min, *Paths to the Triune God: An Encounter between Aquinas and Recent Theologies* (Notre Dame, IN: University of Notre Dame Press, 2005). Henceforth, this article will be referred to as *Min II*.

20. Min I, 87.

21. Min I, 93-94.

22. Jean François Godet Calogeras, "Evangelical Radicalism in the Writings of Francis and Clare of Assisi," in *Vita Evangelica*, edd. Michael Cusato and Jean François Godet-Calogeras (St. Bonaventure, NY: The Franciscan Institute, 2006), 114.

23. For the passages from Alexander of Hales, see *Quaestiones Disputatae: Antequam esset frater* (Quaracchi, Florence: Collegium S. Bonaventurae, 1960), v. I, 97. See also Kenan Osborne, "Alexander of Hales," *The History of Franciscan Theology*, 23-30

24. See Allan B. Wolter, "Duns Scotus and the Existence and Nature of God," 94-130.

25. Kloppenburg, 19-20.

26. This Trinitarian material is based on Section One in the *CCC*, §§1077 to 1109.

27. Luc Mathieu, "Était-il nécessaire que le Christ mourut sur la croix?" *Duns Scot À Paris*, 1302-2002, (Turnhout, Brepols, 2004), 588.

28. Ibid., 584.

29. Johannes Freyer, *Homo Viator: Der Mensch im Lichte des Heilsgeschichte*, 244.

30. See Allan Wolter, "Duns Scotus and the Existence and Nature of God," 116-119.

APPENDIX

The Theology of Salvation

The theology of salvation that is found in the *Catechism of the Catholic Church* does not take into account the complexity of this theme. In almost every theological book on the church, the seven sacraments are presented as a means of salvation. Sacramental liturgy and salvation have a common bond. This bond is expressed in a Trinitarian way at the very beginning of the *Catechism's* focus on the sacramental economy:

The gift of the Spirit ushers in a new era in the "dispensation of the mystery" – the age of the Church, during which Christ manifests, makes present, and communicates his work of salvation through the liturgy of the Church, "until he comes." (§1076)

The liturgy of the church and the work of salvation are united. The Holy Spirit has ushered in this new era, which is an era of salvation, and it is Jesus who manifests and makes salvation present.

The connection of the sacraments to salvation is not in itself a problem. The problem stems from the theological meaning of salvation. In Catholic theological literature there are three different presentations on the meaning of salvation, and all three are acceptable positions. One theological view of salvation is expressed in the phrase, Jesus the Victor. Another theological view of salvation is expressed in the phrase, Jesus the Victim. Still another theological view of salvation is expressed through the phrase, Jesus the Revealer.

In most theological works, the theologies of salvation are presented through the lens of Jesus the Victor, through the lens of Jesus the Victim, or through the lens of Jesus the Revealer. All three theologies of salvation, Victor, Victim, and Revealer, can be found in the scriptures, in church history, and in current theologies of salvation. During the last fifty years, major theologians and church historians have written on the theologies of salvation. Edward Schillebeeckx, J. N. D. Kelly, Gustaf Aulén, Frederick Dillistone, Dieter Wiederkehr, Neil Ormerod, Raymund Schwager, and Anthony Bartlett are only a few of the major authors who have written on the theological issue of salvation as of 2013.

If one sees Jesus as the Victor, then there has to be someone/something over which Jesus is victorious, and Jesus' victory brings about human salvation. If one sees Jesus as the Victim, then there has to be someone or something which caused Jesus to be the victim. When the victim suffers and dies, the acceptance of his victim position allows God to grant us salvation. If one sees Jesus as the revealer, then Jesus' life and death are a revelation of God's gift of salvation. None of these three views has been declared a teaching of the church. All three forms of salvation are acceptable within the Catholic Church.

When one carefully reads the section on salvation in the *Catechism* (§§599-623), one sees that some sentences reflect Jesus the Victor, while other statements reflect Jesus the Victim. Still other passages reflect Jesus the Revealer. The fact that all three theologies of salvation are present in these pages indicates that all three theologies have value. Nonetheless, a conglomerated series of positions on salvation does not produce a clear theological understanding of a theology of salvation. Rather, the conglomerate leaves the reader with a confused notion of what salvation is all about.

In the three forms of salvation mentioned above, there is a key question that challenges each of the three theological views of salvation, and that is that question is the following:

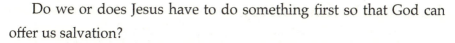

Do we or does Jesus have to do something first so that God can offer us salvation?

This question is extremely important since it opens up the issue of grace freely given. If one has to do something first, then grace is not freely given. Rather, one might argue that it is earned by some form of human action.

Let us consider each of the three theories of salvation and the way in which the theories answer this question.

Jesus The Victor Theory

In this theory, the death of Jesus has been presented over many centuries as a victory of Jesus over death, over sin and over the devil. With the defeat of Satan, our sins can be forgiven and through the crucifixion and resurrection of Jesus, the power of sin and the power of death are also removed.

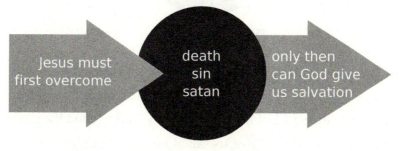

JESUS THE VICTOR THEORY

In this diagram, Jesus must "do" something—namely, conquer death, remove sin and destroy Satan—before God can give us salvation. This seems to be an example of a good-work theology, namely, one must do something first before a gift can be given.

Jesus The Victim Theory

The second theory of salvation is called the victim theory. Jesus offers himself as a victim on the cross and eventually gives up his life. This position was developed in a strong way by Anselm of Canterbury in his book, *Cur Deus Homo*. Anselm wanted nothing to do with a victory understanding of salvation because, in the victory understanding, theologians had written that Satan had rights and that God had to honor the rights of Satan. Anselm stated that Satan had no rights at all, and God did not have to honor any rights that Satan might have. Anselm's victim theory can be outlined as follows:

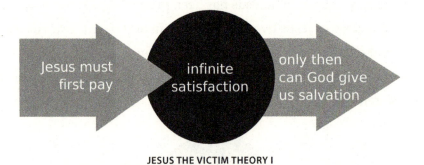

JESUS THE VICTIM THEORY I

In this diagram, the satisfaction theory of St. Anselm's book, *Cur Deus Homo*, is clearly evident. Anselm totally rejected the rights of Satan (the victor theory), but in Anselm's view God needed the payment of satisfaction in order to give us salvation. Marcia Colish, in her volume, *Peter Lombard*, writes:

> Anselm is sensitive to the point that nothing man does can actually increase or diminish God's honor, God being infinite. But the rendering of proper honor to Him expresses a proper attitude in creatures, which contributes to the wholeness and order of the universe. This is the level on which Anselm analyzes the objective side of the transaction, the restoration of honor to God as the service of justice which therefore requires satisfaction as essential.[1]

In the victim theory, human sin can only be taken away when adequate satisfaction is repaid to God. The infinite God requires infinite satisfaction because sin has offended a God who is infinite. Only Jesus can offer infinite satisfaction to the Father so that human sin can be forgiven. This can be diagrammed as follows:

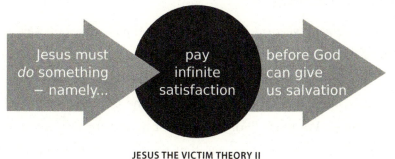

Jesus must *do* something – namely... | pay infinite satisfaction | before God can give us salvation

JESUS THE VICTIM THEORY II

This theory seems to be another example of a good-work theology, in which one must do something first before a gift can be given.

Jesus The Revealer Theory

This theory has had several names; it has also been called a revelatory theory and an illuminative theory. It seems that Peter Lombard was one of its first proponents. John Duns Scotus developed his own explanation of the revealer theory:

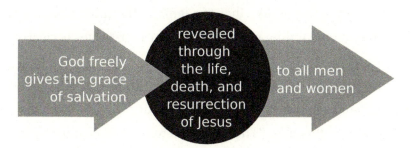

God freely gives the grace of salvation | revealed through the life, death, and resurrection of Jesus | to all men and women

JESUS THE REVEALER THEORY

This theory avoids any trace of a good-work theology. From God's giving to our receiving, the gift of salvation is dependent only on the Giver-God. The theory blends in with the theology of God's grace, namely, that grace is always a gift of God and men and women can do nothing to obtain God's gift of grace.

Closing Remarks

There is a lengthy section in the *Catechism* that focuses on salvation (§§599-623). In the text, God is presented as one to whom all moments of time are present in their immediacy. Therefore, God sees what all men and women will do when he creates the universe and the first human beings. We read: "For the sake of accomplishing his plan of salvation, God permitted the acts that flowed from their blindness" (§600). Evidently, this means that the moment of creation included salvation, since God's plan allowed for the sins of men and women to happen.

However, a plan by God that allows sin is difficult to understand. In the section on the divine plan of salvation, the authors describe the death of Jesus "as a mystery of universal redemption, that is, as the ransom that would free men from slavery of sin" (§601). The *Catechism* also quotes a passage from the First Letter of Peter: "You were ransomed from the futile ways inherited from your fathers ... with the precious blood of Christ, like that of a lamb without blemish or spot" (§602). The understanding of salvation in these passages is clearly Jesus the victim.

In the *Catechism*, there is a title for Section III (§§606-618), namely: "Christ Offered Himself to His Father for Our Sins." In §607, the authors expand on this title: "The desire to embrace his Father's plan of redeeming love inspired Jesus' whole life, for his redemptive passion was the very reason for his Incarnation." This understanding of the death of Jesus is stated even more clearly in §614:

> The sacrifice of Christ is unique; it completes and surpasses all other sacrifices. First, it is a gift from God the Father himself, for the Father handed His Son over to sinners in order to reconcile us with himself. At the same time it is the offering of the Son of God made man, who in freedom and loved offered his life to his Father through the Holy Spirit in reparation for our disobedience.

In §615, the title reads: "Jesus substitutes his obedience for our disobedience." In the text of this paragraph we read: "Jesus atoned for our faults and made satisfaction for our sins to the Father." In §616 we read: "It is love 'to the end' that confers on Christ's sacrifice its value as redemption and reparation, as atonement and satisfaction" In §617, the authors cite a passage from the Council of Trent: "his most holy Passion on the wood of the Cross merited justification for us."

In all of these citations, we hear words which express the Victim theory:

Jesus must "do" something—namely, pay infinite satisfaction—before God can give us salvation.

The Revealer Theory has a major issue which needs further investigation. The difficulty in this third understanding of salvation is its apparent disregard of any contrition on the part of the sinner. God gives salvation to all men and women and there is no mention of a sinner's regret and sorrow. This view seems to eliminate any personal responsibility for the sinful state of their life.

Let me repeat what two Franciscan scholars have written on this subject. The Franciscan theologian, Luc Mathieu, in his essay "Était-il nécessaire que le Christ mourût sur la croix?" carefully explains this inter-relationship of creation and incarnation:

> God's pardon of sin is an act of pure gratuity and pure benevolence which is intrinsic to the act of creation... There is no other necessity than the divine free will, God's gratuitous

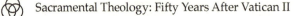

love, and God' omnipotence.[2]

Was it necessary that humanity be restored and that Christ had to suffer? It is fitting that we never forget that the divine act of creation is gratuitous, just as all actions of God ad extra.[3]

The Franciscan theologian, Johannes Freyer, mentions that the Franciscan theologians of the thirteenth century developed a unique soteriology. Franciscan soteriology is based on the Trinitarian God who is *bonum sui diffusivum* (Bonaventure) and based on the infinite free and loving will of God (Scotus).[4]

All three theological forms of salvation are mentioned in the section of the *Catechism* that focuses on salvation. This co-mingling of three different and even opposing theologies of salvation that are found in the *Catechism* does not and cannot offer the reader a clear theological understanding of the term salvation.

At the beginning of the twenty-first century, theologians are still trying to formulate a satisfactory interpretation of God's plan of salvation. As we have seen, the three theological theories of redemption described above are all mentioned in the section of the *Catechism* that deals with Christ's redemptive death. The *Catechism's* presentation of salvation includes references to all three of the above theories (§§ 599-623). In the *Catechism's* presentation of the seven sacraments, the three theological theories on salvation are also operative. The lack of a clear theological stance on the meaning of salvation still baffles the Christian world.

John Nilson states that "Vatican II recovered the more traditional and comprehensive meaning of salvation as transformation of the entire universe." This transformation of the theology of salvation is present in the Pastoral Constitution in the Modern World.[5] In *Gaudium et Spes*, one reads:

> In pursuing its own salvific purpose not only does the church communicate divine life to humanity but in a certain sense it casts the reflected light of that divine life over all the earth, notably in the way it heals and elevates the dignity of the human person, in the way it consolidates society and endows people's daily activity with a deeper sense and meaning (§40).

The bishops of Vatican II are viewing the way in which the church should ideally be present throughout today's world. Too often the church is not casting a reflection of divine life over all the earth. For instance, Liberation Theology pleaded with the leaders of the church to take into account the cultural beauty of many populations on this earth. This plea has only achieved some small beginnings of cultural acceptance. Feminist theology has pleaded with the leaders of the church to allow women to be more involved in the mission of the church. To some degree this plea has been heard, but there is still a strong hesitation to allow Catholic women in ecclesiastical areas of serious import.

When we consider salvation outside the Roman Catholic Church, there was and still is a major point of theological disagreement. In the *Catechism*, there is a section entitled "Outside the Church there is no salvation" (§§846-848). The authors attempt to provide us with a statement which is "positively reformulated." The reformulation, however, is unclear since the text includes these words: "all salvation comes from Christ the Head through the Church which is the Body" (§846). All salvation, accordingly, is Christ-centered and Church-centered.

In the last fifty years since Vatican II, the theology of salvation has been richly discussed. We see this development not only in the conciliar documents but also in the *Catechism of the Catholic Church* and in sundry statements which the Vatican Curia has published. Today, the theology of salvation has taken a major step forward, since theologians are now beginning to acknowledge that God's salvation extends to women and men who belong to denominations of the Christian religion beyond the Roman Catholic community, or who belong to the Eastern religious communities, and even to those who are not Christian, some of whom are members of non-Christian religions. This outward movement of salvation is evident, but as of today a clear and comprehensive presentation of the theology of salvation remains in its infancy.

Endnotes

1. Marcia Colish, *Peter Lombard*, (Leiden: Brill, 1994), 452.

2. Mathieu, "Était-il nécessaire que le Christ mourut sur la croix?" *Duns Scot À Paris*, 588.

3. Ibid., 584.

4. Freyer, *Homo Viator: Der Mensch im Lichte des Heilsgeschichte*, 244.

5. John Nilson, "Salvation," in the *HarperCollins Encyclopedia of Catholicism*, 1159.

Bibliography

Aland, Kurt. *Did the Early Church Baptize Infants?* Eng. trans. by G. R. Beasley Murray. Philadelphia: Westminster, 1963.

Bardy, Gustave. *A l'école de saint Augustin*. Ecully: Oeuvre Populaire d'Education, 1947.

Barnes, Michel René. "Latin Trinitarian Theology." *The Cambridge Companion to the Trinity*. New York: Cambridge University Press, 2011.

Baraúna, William, ed. *The Liturgy of Vatican II*. Chicago: Franciscan Herald Press, 1966.

Battifol, Pierre, *Études d'histoire et de théologie positive*. Paris: V. Lecoffre, 1902.

Bausch, William. *A New Look at the Sacraments*. Mystic, CN: Twenty-Third Publications, 1983.

Boudinhon, August. "Sur l'histoire de la pénitence, à propos d'un livre recent." *Revue d'histoire et literature religieuse*, 2, 1897.

Bourque, Emmanuel. *Histoire de la Pénitence-Sacrement*. Quebec: Laval University Press, 1947.

Chauvet, Louis-Marie. *Symbole et Sacrement: Un relecture sacramentelle de l'existence chrétienne*. Paris. Les Éditions du Cerf, 1987.

Ciferni, Andrew. "Anointing of the Sick." *The HarperCollins Encyclopedia of Catholicism*, ed. Richard McBrien. San Francisco: HarperSanFrancisco, 1995.

Colish, Marcia. *Peter Lombard*. Leiden: Brill, 1994.

Colombo, Carlo. "The Hierarchical Structure of the Church." *Vatican II: An Interfaith Appraisal*. Notre Dame, IN: University of Notre Dame Press, 1966.

Cooke, Bernard. *Ministry to Word and Sacrament*. Philadelphia: Fortress Press, 1976.

D'Arcy, M. J. ed. *A Monument to Saint Augustine*. London, Sheed and Ward, 1950.

De Régnon, Theodore. *Études de théologie positive sur la sainte Trinité*. Paris: Victor Retaux et fils, 1892.

Duffy, Regis. *Real Presence*. San Francisco: Harper & Row, 1982.

Freyer, Johannes. *Homo Viator: Der Mensch im Lichte der Heislgeschichte*. Kevalaer: Verlag Butzon & Bercker, 2001.

Gilbert, Paul. *Introducción a la Teología Medieval*. Estella-Navarra: Editorial Verbo Divino, 1993.

Gilson, Étienne. *Introduction à l'étude de saint Augustin*. Paris. J. Vrin, 1949.

Godet-Calogeras, Jean François. "Evangelical Radicalism in the Writings of Francis and Clare of Assisi." *Vita Evangelica*. St. Bonaventure, NY: The Franciscan Institute, 2006.

Gonzalez, Olegario. *Misterio Trinitario y existencia humana: studio histórico teología en torno a San Buenaventura*. Madrid: Ediciones Rialp, 1965.

Hammerman, Nora, ed. *Saint Augustine: Father of European and African Civilization*. New York: Benjamin Franklin House, 1985.

Hayes, Zachary. "Introduction." *Works of St. Bonaventure: Disputed Questions on the Mystery of the Trinity*. St. Bonaventure, NY: The Franciscan Institute, 1979.

Hunt, Anne. *Trinity: Nexus of the Mysteries of Christian Faith*. Maryknoll, NY: Orbis, 2005.

Jeremias, Joachim. *Infant Baptism in the First Four Centuries*. Eng. trans. by D. Caines. London: SCM Press, 1960.

— *The Origin of Infant Baptism*. Eng. trans. by Dorothea M. Barton. London: SCM Press, 1963.

Kevane, Eugene. *Augustine and Educator: A Study in the Fundamentals of Christian Formation*. Wesminster, MD: Newman Press, 1964.

Kirsch, P. A. *Zur Geschiche der katholischen Beichte*. Würzburg: Gobel und Scherer, 1902.

Kloppenburg, Bonaventure. *A Eclesiologia do Vaticano*. Petropolis: Editora Vozes Limitada, 1971. Eng. trans. by Matthew J O'Connell, *The Ecclesiology of Vatican II*. Chicago: Franciscan Herald Press, 1974.

Lea, Henry C. *A History of Auricular Confession and Indulgences in the Latin Church*. Philadephia: Lea Bros. & Co., 1896.

Leahy, Thomas. "The Epistle of James." *The New Jerome Biblical Commentary*. Englewood Cliffs, NJ: Prentice Hall, 1990.

Lennerz Heinrich. "Das Konzil von Trient und theologische Schulmeinungen." *Scholastik*, 4, 1929.

Loofs, F. *Leitfaden zum Studium der Dogmengeschichte*. 4 vv. Leipzig: Halle Niemeier, 1906.

Mathieu, Luc. "Était-il nécessaire que le Christ mourût?" *Duns Scot À Paris,*

1302-2002. Turnhout, Brepols, 2004.

Meyer, John. "Jesus of History." *The New Jerome Biblical Commentary*. Englewood Cliffs, NJ: Prentice Hall, 1990.

Miller, John H. ed. *Vatican II: An Interfaith Appraisal*. Notre Dame, IN: University of Notre Dame Press, 1966.

Min, Anselm Kyongsuk. "God as the mystery of sharing and shared love: Thomas Aquinas on the Trinity" *The Cambridge Companion to the Trinity*. New York: Cambridge University Press, 2011, ed. Peter Phan.

— *Paths to the Triune God: An Encounter between Aquinas and Recent Theologies*. Notre Dame, IN: University of Notre Dame Press, 2005.

Moeller, Charles. "History of *Lumen Gentium's* Structure and Ideas." *Vatican II: An Interfaith Appraisal*. Notre Dame, IN: University of Notre Dame Press, 1966.

Nairn, Thomas, ed. *The Franciscan Moral Vision: Responding to God's Love*. St. Bonaventure, NY: Franciscan Institute Publications, 2013.

Nilson, John. "Salvation." *The HarperCollins Encyclopedia of Catholicism*. San Francisco: HarperSanFrancisco, 1995.

Oates, Whitney J. *Basic Writings of Saint Augustine*. New York: Random House, 1948.

O'Meara, Thomas. *Thomas Aquinas: Theologian*. Notre Dame, IN: University of Notre Dame Press, 1997.

Osborne, Kenan. *A Theology of the Church for the Third Millennium: A Franciscan Approach*. Leiden: Brill, 2009.

— *Sacramental Theology: A General Introduction*. Mahwah, NJ: Paulist, 1988.

— *The Christian Sacraments of Initiation*. Mahwah, NJ: Paulist, 1987.

— *Reconciliation and Justification: The Sacrament and its Theology*. Mahwah, NJ: Paulist, 1990.

— *Priesthood: A History of the Ordained Ministry in the Roman Catholic Church*. Mahwah, NJ: Paulist, 1988.

— *Sacramental Guidelines: A Companion to the New Catechism for Religious Educators*. Mahwah, NJ: Paulist, 1995.

Phan, Peter, ed. *The Cambridge Companion to the Trinity*. New York: Cambridge University Press, 2011.

Philips, Gerard. "The Church: Mystery and Sacrament." *Vatican II: An Interfaith Appraisal*. Notre Dame, IN: University of Notre Dame Press, 1966.

Rahner, Karl. *Kirche und Sakramente*. Freiburg im B.: Herder, 1963. Eng. trans. by W. J. O'Hara, *The Church and the Sacraments*. New York: Herder and

Herder, 1963.

Rahner, Karl. "Zur Theologie des Symbols." *Schriften zur Theologie*, IV. Einseideln: Benziger Verlag, 1962.

Saliverri, Ioachim, ed. *Sacrae Theologiae Summa*. Madrid: Biblioteca de Autores Cristianos, 1962.

Schillebeeckx, Edward. *Christus: Sacrament van de Godsonmoeting*. Bilthoven: H. Nelissen, 1960. Eng. trans. by Cornelius Ernst, *Christ the Sacrament of the Encounter with God*. New York: Sheed and Ward, 1963.

Segundo, Juan Luis. *The Sacraments Today*. Maryknoll, NY: Orbis, 1974.

Semmelroth, Otto. *Vom Sinn der Sakramente*. Frankfurt am M: Verlag Josef Knecht, 1960. Eng. trans. by Emily Schossberger. *Church and Sacrament*. Notre Dame, IN: Fides Publishers, 1965.

Strauss, Gerhard. *Schriftgebrauch, Schriftauslegung, und Schriftbeweis bei Augustin*. Tübingen: J. C. B. Mohr, 1959.

Umberg, Johann B. "Die Bewertung der Trienter Lehren durch Pius VI." *Scholastik*, 4, 1929.

Vacandard, Elphège. *La pénitence publique dans l'Église*. Paris: Bloud, 1903.

Wainwright, Elaine. "Like a finger pointing to the moon: exploring the Trinity in/ and the New Testament." *The Cambridge Companion to the Trinity*. New York: Cambridge University Press, 2011.

White, John T. *Latin-English and English-Latin Dictionary*. Chicago: Follert, 1928.

Wolter, Allan. "Duns Scotus and the Existence and Nature of God." *Proceedings of the American Philosophical Association*. Washington, DC: The Catholic University of America Press, 1954.

CPSIA information can be obtained at www.ICGtesting.com
Printed in the USA
BVOW08s2046290116

434468BV00003B/196/P